Hey, Bub!

Two Brothers and a Chromosome to Spare

STEVEN PRATER

 FriesenPress

Suite 300 - 990 Fort St
Victoria, BC, V8V 3K2
Canada

www.friesenpress.com

ISBN
978-1-4602-8908-2 (Hardcover)
978-1-4602-8909-9 (Paperback)
978-1-4602-8910-5 (eBook)

1. BIOGRAPHY & AUTOBIOGRAPHY, PEOPLE WITH DISABILITIES

Distributed to the trade by The Ingram Book Company

TABLE OF CONTENTS

INTRODUCTION

"Mrs. Prater, I need to inform you that your baby is a Mongoloid idiot."

That was how the stunning, sobering conversation started with my mom's doctor shortly after the birth of her second son, Tom. My dad was not present at that meeting so Elsie Prater, age twenty-five, had to digest that short, blunt message on her own.

A conversation like this has been spoken a million times to a million parents. Medical staff have watched the countenances of the new or expectant parents come crashing down. Today, they will use the accepted medical term "Down syndrome," but the message is still the same, as are the responses.

Currently four hundred thousand people in the United States are affected with Down syndrome, and it is found in one in seven hundred pregnancies.[1] Scientists say that Down syndrome is a genetic anomaly caused by the extra splitting of the twenty-first chromosome during the early stages of embryonic formation in a mother's womb. This mutation creates certain characteristics that are linked to arrested physical and mental growth, and it bestows a familial appearance to those who have the extra chromosome.

Although a serious matter, it doesn't have to be a tragedy of epic proportions. Many people with Down's live active, fulfilling lives and make significant contributions to society. They often make our environment a happier, more humane, and gentler place to live. Families and neighbors may need to adapt to what is now termed a "developmental/mental disability," but usually these accommodations are less than they fear and many quickly admit that there is a net gain in quality of life when all the chips have been counted. Down syndrome folks usually enrich the lives of their families, neighbors, and people with whom they come in contact.

Tests have been available for decades that can be administered to an expectant mother to determine if her fetus carries this extra chromosome. Such tests open questions about whether or not the pregnancy should be terminated. With the results of amniocentesis, many parents choose to abort their babies. This decision must be gut-wrenching. Others choose to go ahead with their pregnancies and play the hand that has been dealt. This too is a difficult choice, knowing that their family will need to make sacrifices to accommodate a child with potentially significant limitations.

Amniocentesis was not available to my parents in the late 1940s. The procedure wasn't safely perfected until the late 1960s for prenatal screening purposes. In 1949, you didn't know what you got until you got it. It is disconcerting to know, though, that forms of infanticide were still in common practice at the time of my brother's birth to deal with the unwanted in our society. Parents who had just given birth to a child with a severe physical or mental disability were frequently encouraged to leave their newborn baby behind with medical staff who, depending on the severity of the disability, might then withhold medical care or nourishment.

In 1949, Elsie and Merle Prater were shocked to learn that their second child had an extra chromosome. They sensed something was amiss soon after birth, and it was confirmed by the doctors that Thomas Alan Prater had Down syndrome. My folks were heartbroken. They knew that their growing family would now have a child with serious health issues and constraints. They knew they would be custodial parents of Tom until either he died or they did. I am grateful that my parents chose to hang on to their second son. It made our family closer and stronger in many ways.

During those first several months, Mom and Dad struggled to tell anyone about the diagnosis, even their parents, due to lingering societal taboos. However, their little secret was hard to conceal, as it had enough telltale symptoms to eventually reveal itself. After about five gripping months of grief, confusion, and fear, Elsie returned to her parents' home in Iowa for a visit. Face to face with her mother, she was finally able to tell the truth about Tommy.

Rose Jansen said, "I always knew something was the matter with Tom."

Incredulous, Elsie responded, "How did you know?"

"It's been five months since he was born and you've barely spoken a word about him," Rose replied.

Elsie and Merle finally exhaled. They then began the journey of speaking of Tom to family and friends and recharting their course for their own expectations, as well as how to raise their growing post-war family.

Tom was welcomed not only by our nuclear family, but also by grandparents, aunts, uncles, cousins, friends, neighbors, and just about anyone who met him. He was accepted for who he was, not his disability. He caught a few stares from time to time, but I was never aware of him

being treated maliciously. Some may have been a bit condescending, but that is understandable.

Tom had a real personality; he thought and reasoned, he
communicated (not very well verbally, but impressively in
other ways). He had a great sense of humor (especially slap-
stick), followed instructions, and knew how to empathize
with others. He could receive and give love like no one I
have ever known. It was as if he emitted "love rays." His life
had a few tragic turns, which he heroically survived, but
mostly he embodied delighted happiness. When given a
wrapped present to open for a birthday, he owned the word
glee. To watch a human body scrunch itself up and then
explode in two-year-old, unwavering joy is not something
many people can do. I'm honored to have witnessed such
joyful abandon most of my life.

Tom's life was important, but outside of the circle
of friends and family, his influence stopped there. His
recorded story also may have stopped there, had a childhood friend not responded to a Facebook picture I had
posted of my nuclear family. The shot was taken a few years
after Tom's death, so he was obviously not in the portrait.
His absence in the photo did not prevent my friend from
asking the innocent question, "Whatever happened to
Tom?" At that moment, I realized that a part of his story
needed to be told so that others might enjoy and learn
from this very special brother. It is from my viewpoint, as a
younger sibling, that these memories are recounted.

Tom was every bit a man and a member of our society,
as much as anyone was—he just spoke a slightly different
language and lived at a different speed. Sometimes I was
aware of his being radically different from me, but usually
he was amazingly, boringly similar. I hope these stories of
where our everyday lives intersected will help celebrate and
honor his.

I have often wondered what it would have been like had
Tom been one of us "regulars." I usually don't get far into

my musings before I come to the realization that it couldn't have been any better than it was, just as he was.

I have already used the term "Mongoloid" in this introduction and I need to clarify some terminology and intent. "Down syndrome" has not always been the politically nor medically correct term for this condition. The label has changed at least a couple of times over my lifetime. My parents were told, "Mongoloid idiot," and I grew up with the terms "Mongoloid" and "Mongoloidism" ("Mongolism" is actually the correct term). I frequently used these to describe my brother until 1977, when a doctor in Rochester, Minnesota, informed me of how inappropriate it was. However, in the 1950s and '60s, it was still an acceptable and even a clinical term. I do not use it any longer except in its historical context. I will explain this more later.

I have also used the term "mentally retarded" when I have wanted to be more generic and didn't want to get into the specifics of Down syndrome. "Retarded" has been a more inclusive term of what is now regarded as a "mental or intellectual disability." Alas, "retarded" has also become an increasingly pejorative and demeaning word along with its now definitely derogatory root, "retard." The term "mental retardation" may still be okay to use in some circles, but I'm skittish. The point is that when we broach this topic over the course of a specific era, terms may get used that were once acceptable, but now are not. As I use these terms, I pray you take them in the historical context in which they are offered. I do not intend to use any of these words to derogate persons who may have capabilities different from mine.

ACKNOWLEDGMENT

This book would never have been written, nor even started, if it were not for the encouragement of my wife, Dorothy (Dot) Prater. She read and commented on draft after draft and was ruthless (in a gentle sort of way) with her proposed edits. She seemed to chuckle, or at least crack a smile, at the right places, so that kept me going when I thought about quitting.

Dot missed out on the first twenty-five years of Tom's life, but she picked up on his last thirty-four, so she too shares a wonderful history with my brother. Along with wielding a wicked blue pencil, she was also able to add many interesting side-bars to the story of his life.

To Elsie E. Prater, better known to me as Mom. Elsie passed away on January 1, 2016, between the writing and publication of this book.

CHAPTER 1

The Beginnings

On the eighth day God said, "Let there be marshmallows."
Then He said, "OMH (Oh, My Human!), I think I made a big mistake!"
The eighth day was quickly expunged.

2 Genesis 1:15-16

Tommy was two when he welcomed his younger brother into the family, making the Prater boys a new force to be reckoned with in the neighborhood. He now split the difference between the oldest, Jeff, and me, the skinny, bald, wrinkled screamer.

I moved into the boys' barracks in a small home my folks rented a couple of miles south of the hamlet of Vestal, New York. Vestal was a suburb, in the loosest sense of the term, of the Triple Cities of Endicott, Johnson City, and Binghamton; all relatively small cities developed along the Susquehanna River and a stone's throw from the Pennsylvania border. Our house was on Landen Road and it had a creek in the back yard and a busy Route 26 in the front—everything a young child could ever dream of for a playground. The little enclave of maybe a dozen houses was squeezed in between hills in every direction and had a little feeling of *not* suburbia. If this neighborhood was not a part of Appalachia proper, perhaps it was a suburb of it, as well.

I don't remember much of the Landen Road house, as my first vivid memories start after the family moved to the two-story, four-square house on Melbourne Street (in Vestal proper). This was the first house my parents owned. I must have been about three and a half, as I remember my sister, Nancy, as an infant. At eight years old, Jeff needed more privacy (I guess) and Nancy, being the only girl, undoubtedly needed her own room. With Mom and Dad in the third bedroom, this left only one more room, with two kids to share it. My room assignment came up with Tom's name on it.

Tom and I were pretty good bunkmates. He didn't talk much and I took his few peculiar habits and mannerisms in stride. His language was simple and when he spoke, it was usually only a word or two, and then only a close approximation of English. His words were more guttural and muted and can be replicated if one jams about half a dozen marshmallows into one's mouth. All of his utterances tended to run together, making his language more than a little cryptic for the uninitiated. He was able to communicate basic needs, and understood much more than he could linguistically convey. I came to understand most of his monosyllabic words or grunts pretty well. Although my own language skills rapidly outpaced Tom's, I developed a strong preference for speaking with marshmallows in my mouth.

Tom also had a bit of a strange look. In addition to eyes that crossed a little, they were somewhat slanted and he liked to stick his tongue out frequently. I noticed that he moved a lot slower than me, or anyone else I knew at the ripe old age of five. He walked with his head down and plodded. I also noticed that other people took double-takes at him when we were out in public and looked at him as if something was wrong. I might have been six when Mom explained to me that he was "retarded" and that he was a "Mongoloid."

Back in the 1950s, "Mongoloid" was an acceptable (actually clinical) term for having Down syndrome, which is a genetic anomaly that creates a condition whereby each cell has forty-seven chromosomes rather than the normal forty-six (twenty-three pairs—half from the mother, half from the father). It wasn't until the 1970s that "Down syndrome" became the more accepted name of this condition (an alternate term uses the possessive form of Down's syndrome).

John Langdon Down, for whom the condition is named, was an English physician of the mid-1800s. He dedicated his life to the study and care of "Mongolian idiots" and is credited as the first person to etiologically classify these persons.[2] Within the general population of what he clinically labeled "idiots," he noticed similar features such as broad faces, short noses, thick tongues, fat lips, and slanted eyes. He drew comparisons with the eastern Asian race and postulated that these Asian-looking people of Caucasian parents, due to some heredity hiccup, had reverted and connected to a lower, less intelligent race (of course the Caucasian race was at the top of the heap!).[3] In the mid-1970s, persons of East Asian descent (real Mongols) took umbrage at a genetic defect associated with idiocy[*] being

---

[*] "Idiot" was an old English term that came to take on legal significance as it referred to a person lacking intellectual abilities advanced enough to care for themselves. It connoted a permanent condition from birth. The term, "lunatic" described a person of unsound mind who may experience moments of lucidity and then the next moment be totally irrational. People with Down syndrome would have been clinically classified as "idiots." Through the 1950s, they were clinically known as "Mongol idiots."

named after them.[4] Representatives from Mongolia took their cause to the powers that be and the association between a genetic condition and an intelligent race was officially dropped.

Although Down syndrome had been presumed to be a genetic disorder since the nineteenth century, it wasn't until 1959 that a French physician and his small team were able to separate, stain, and photograph human chromosomes and definitively identify the triplet configuration of chromosome number twenty-one of Mongoloid children.[5] Jérôme Lejeune had found the genetic link causing Mongolism. He renamed it "Trisomy vingt-et-une" (Trisomy twenty-one), a synonymous title for Down syndrome still predominantly used in France.[6] With this discovery, along with techniques to safely retrieve amniotic fluid from a pregnant mother's womb, conclusive, scientific prenatal screening began.[7] So opened Pandora's Box for the potential termination of Down's fetuses.

Okay, so I didn't get all that back story when I was six. Heck, they hadn't even made the chromosomal discovery yet. Not only that, but I didn't care. All I really wanted to know was if Tom was different or not. He was. No big deal; Mongoloid, retarded, whatever. Looking back, it was probably a good time for me to learn a little about Tom's condition. It was informative, but the knowledge in no way upset me nor derailed my relationship with my brother.

Tom understood a lot more than he could relate. This worked out well for a lot of our (my) schemes. He also admitted guilt easily so this was a perfect set up for an accomplice and an accomplice's need for a sound alibi. The folks also made some allowances for him, so by association, I was often handed a more lenient punishment when culprits were found and discipline needed to be meted out.

Did I manipulate an overly compliant partner with my extra-legal adventures? You bet I did! Tom was easy pickins' and while I was not learning many hard negotiating skills with my peers or oldest brother (you cannot argue and win with a brother four years older), I was learning how to deceive and exploit another's weakness. I'm sure this was not a surprise to my parents as they watched our antics. I remember well-directed admonitions to not take advantage of Tom's extremely naïve and willing nature.

In the early years, we were basically twin cat burglars. Nothing big, mostly petty larceny. We'd go after graham crackers, candy bars, cookies, and that kind of entry level crime. We became adept at finding where Mom hid sweets and would go to dangerous extents to secure them. A favorite spot for loot was a high cupboard above the kitchen sink. To extract these treasures required careful timing, cunning, balance, and a hefty dose of stupidity—all of which Tom and I could readily supply.

Early one Saturday morning, Tom and I put together a spontaneous raiding party. While the rest of the house was still sleeping, we quietly snuck downstairs to the kitchen. Climbing onto a kitchen chair, I was able to gain access to the counter top. Risking life and limb, I side-shuffled in my Dr. Denton PJ's, carefully reaching above me for the cupboard that might contain our treat. Tiptoeing on that two inch piece of Formica between the edge of the sink and eternity and balancing myself with one hand, I made exploratory gropes in the cupboard with my other. Ah hah! A plastic bag, soft and spongy.

"Ka-ching!"

Small fingers deftly plucked the bag out, dropping it to my waiting get-away man. A whole bag of Jet-Puffed marshmallows to split 50-50 (or 90-10, whatever I thought fair). I remember sneaking the spoils back to our bedroom, where we began an intensive program of sugar inhalation. We may have been enjoying our ill-gotten goods a little too boisterously, though, as I remember the pajama-clad sheriff busting into our bedroom to find guilty souls with mouths full of white goo. Fortunately, Tom broke into his infectious I'm-as-guilty-as-sin laugh and his self-incriminating, "No! No! No!" We got off easy. We were given suspended sentences and ordered to do community service by returning the remaining two or three marshmallows to the authorities.

That particular cupboard was rarely used again for such storage without proper administrative surveillance. However, with careful espionage and "counter intelligence," Tom and I would continue to find new caches around the kitchen in upper cabinets.

Tom also taught me how to "Bah." Bah-ing was a drug free, non-habit-forming method of self-medication to combat insomnia. When bedtime rolled around at 7:00 or 7:30 p.m. (way too early, even when I couldn't tell time), Tom and I were not usually ready for actual sleep. No one in civilized society was ready to go to bed at that time, let alone try to sleep. To promote somnolence, we'd try jumping on beds, which normally lasted only a few seconds before a verbal reproof would come floating up the stairs: "STOP THE JUMPING!"

Our bedtime conversations were even shorter as Tom, no matter how hard he may have tried, just wasn't much into discussions. Bored, we'd lay down and try to fall asleep—nothin' doing. I don't know where Tom learned it, but somehow he figured out that if he laid face down on his bed and starting making an "aah" sound that, he could bounce his head into the pillow to made this wonderful "bah, bah, bah." What a wonderful discovery. It was a pure stroke of genius! Soon there were two of us "bah-ing" away like a corral of crazed sheep. If this self-pacification did the trick, within a couple of minutes, we'd both be out cold. On the other hand, if it kept going for fifteen minutes, then another reprisal was shouted out, "STOP THE BAH-ING," and strict silence would be observed for maybe thirty seconds. If we heard footsteps on the stair, we were both sound asleep before the bedroom door opened.

Another regular occurrence in the bedroom was the presence of Vick's VapoRub. A typical characteristic of Down's folks is a high palate that extends the roof of the mouth up into the nasal passages, thus reducing some of the sinus cavities. In addition, Tom had a deviated septum that conspired, with the high palate, to give him congestion problems. Whenever he got a little stuffed-up or got a nasty cough, in rolled The Vaporizer. This was basically a steam kettle that sat on the floor into which Mom put water and copious amounts of the gelatinous, eye watering, mentholated petroleum distillate everyone has come to know and love. They still make the stuff, but I think it is intended to rub on the inflicted party's chest so the fumes will rise and work their magic. Mom, however, seemed to believe that the entire room needed to be fumigated. Consequently, a glob of this petro-chemical was floated on the steaming boiling water and the atmosphere in the room would turn into a dark foggy night, right out of a street scene from Sherlock Holmes. My eyes would water and each inhaled breath would be like trying to take a deep breath in sub-zero temperatures. Every little nostril hair would twitch and lung alveoli would quiver. In the morning after a proper fumigation, the windows would be coated with glop. I believe we enjoyed doodling on the glass panes through the grease residue left behind. One thing I knew for certain was that there was no sign of nasal mucus build-up anywhere within a two block radius. If the practice of boiling mentholated grease in an unsupervised child's bedroom was not recommended, it worked pretty well anyway.

Tom and I also shared the heating register in the winter. The floor register closest to the basement furnace was in the dining room, just around the corner from the living room. It was a twelve inch square, cast metal grate composed of one-inch square openings and because it was the first stop on the furnace duct run, it pumped out the warmest heat of any register in the house. On a cold winter morning, this was the toastiest place in the house, aside from being under the covers. Our butts were little enough that we could usually share the register together. I may have gotten a little more grate space, as Tom was not aware of floor register parity. Getting more didn't seem to matter much to him so long as he got some (is this a great brother or what?). Having Tom around taught all of us kids to share more freely. I believe it is characteristic of most Down's persons to not be overly possessive or covetous about most things. What a wonderful little role model for a younger brother to follow.

We would sit on the grate and look at picture books, or find some crayons to use in coloring books or picture books—or walls. We would use whatever canvas we could find within reach to convey our youthful yearnings for our artistic expression. The cave-wall writing phase was short-lived.

Our tenure on the register depended on several things. The biggest threat was an older brother or a younger sister. If Jeff got up early and wanted it, it was his—and his alone. He'd grab a chapter book and give us the older brother look to scram, and then hog the whole square, soaking up every stinking bit of heat. Then he'd gloat.

When Nancy was old enough, she started to elbow her way in. If she wanted it, she'd start whining until we yielded our toasted buns for her frozen one. Did Tom ever get implicated in her accusations? No! Just me. Why?

"MOOOOOMMM, Steve's hogging the whole register and won't share!"

"MOOOOOMMM, Steve's making faces at me and won't let me sit on the register!"

"MOOOOOMMM, Steve's dropping all my crayons down the register!"

"MOOOOOMMM, Steve's breathing!"

"Okay, I was going to give it to her anyway."

That floor register was one of life's simple pleasures. There is nothing like a hot, red, waffle-stamped hiney to start a cold winter day. I believe that most of the world's problems would be solved if we could provide a warm twelve inch square for every man, woman, and child on the planet.

Tom and I continued to develop at roughly the same rate. We were like twins until I was about four. Mom would even make identical outfits for us as some sort of fashion statement. Then it seemed that my cognitive development kept growing rapidly, while Tom's slowed to a crawl. His motor skills plateaued and although he continued to grow physically (albeit at a slower pace), I began to don the mantel of leadership between us.

Speech was always difficult for Tom and for him to get out more than three or four syllables at a time was hard. One of the longest phrases we ever heard him say was his word "Memigooie." Phonetically it would be pronounced pretty much like I wrote it: mem-mee-goo-ee. It was an astounding four syllables long. After a couple of excruciating months trying to decipher what it meant, the family finally determined its meaning to be, "May I be excused, please?" That short sentence, I believe, is an ancient phrase that was employed when a) families had dinner together at the same table and at the same time; b) it was expected that you ask permission to leave the table when you were finished with your meal; and c) it gave you license to leave so quickly that you didn't get stuck clearing or washing dishes.

Most of Tom's language consisted of simple, one or two syllable words, completely devoid of verbs, nouns, adverbs, adjectives, and even those pesky articles. Because of my early association with Tom's primitive language skills, I personally blame him for my inability to analytically diagram a sentence. Seriously, my language skills were probably slowed by having my first-mate for the first four years of my life unable to speak our mother tongue effectively. I don't know how typical this is in other families, but I'm guessing it varies wildly with factors such as age between siblings, parental intervention, preschool opportunities, and a child's normal disposition to learn language skills.

Nonetheless, Tom was able to express his needs and make his desires known. For example, a need to take a bathroom break was requested as "Tink." All it took was for someone to say, "Okay Tom, go." However, if no one was paying attention and permission was not granted, the request would be made again with a demonstration of urgency accompanied with the reminiscence of a familiar gas aroma to reinforce the need.

When our children were in grade school they made the discovery that Tom had learned how to communicate this through sign language as well. Our kids all attended a magnet school for children with hearing disabilities, so everyone in Ann Sullivan School learned American Sign Language, even if they did not have a hearing problem. One day while we were visiting, Tommy held up his hand in a fist with his thumb between his forefinger and middle finger and gave it a little shake. This is the symbol for the letter T. One of our kids, without hesitation, said, "I think Tommy has to go to the bathroom." Sure enough, a potty break was on his *immediate* agenda.

Tom's motor skills were also arrested. Stubby fingers, shorter limbs, and weaker muscle tone, common to most Down syndrome folks, conspired to make Tom seem like he was always riding the brakes. Like his speech, his manual dexterity slowed to about a three-year-old's level. That said, Tom considered himself a master puzzler. Wooden jig-saw puzzles with a half dozen or so painted pieces with the little handles on them were his favorite. Mom always had a stack of these for Tom to do. They were his brain teasers. They kept him sharp, on his toes, and out of trouble.

He'd take a puzzle, dump out the pieces, and then go about trying to rearrange them back into the cut-out forms on the board. Each piece would be twisted and turned, inverted, tested, and retested for fit. The idea of actually matching the shapes was a little advanced for him. Even in his late fifties, the concept of abstracting shapes and forms was complex. It mattered little, though, as he would eventually solve these spatial problems. He got the puzzle back together by brutalizing each piece until, by force, they ran out of options and dropped in. Even when we were much older, Nancy and I often sat on the floor with him and worked on putting our own puzzles together. Tom liked the camaraderie and we enjoyed doing something with him that he liked to do.

When I was about ten, I was given a puzzle of the United States. It helped me to learn the geography of our country and know that (pay attention kids and wives) Maryland is NOT next to Maine, even though they may both be on the right-hand coast (I believe they call the Atlantic Ocean). I became pretty darn good at putting that baby together and I set a high standard for my younger sister. Tom, on the other hand, could only get about half of the states to fit in the cut-out of the cardboard country. California would be in the middle of the country, Montana down in the Florida neighborhood, New York might be in the southwest somewhere, and Texas would have been ceded to the Pacific Ocean. Tom's perception of the United States was about as big a mess as it is today. With Tom's revisionist cartography, Thomas Jefferson would have gotten a whole lot less real estate with the Louisiana Purchase and Lewis and Clark would still be looking for a passage to the Pacific. In Tom's map, there would have been room for only five of the original thirteen colonies. "I'm terribly sorry, Virginia, but you didn't make the cut. Try again next week."

Although his speech was impaired and his cognition slowed, he could understand and do many things. Tom was able to dress himself (a little help with the buttons, please), do most of his bathroom chores, and would faithfully follow simple instructions.

"Tom, please put the plates around the dinner table."

"Tommy, go find the chocolate chips and bring them back to the bedroom."

"Tom, take off your socks and put them in the hamper." (My wife hopes I'll learn this task someday.)

This willingness to please could occasionally work against me, as he did not always differentiate whose instructions to follow. I recall a specific incident in November, 1970. I had just finished my first quarter at the university and I was sleeping-in, trying to catch up on some cramming induced lack of shut eye. Mom, thinking that noon was late enough, had a different opinion about how much sleep I needed. She coerced Tom into a traitorous mission. Faithfully obeying her orders, he shuffled up the steps to the second floor and let himself into my bedroom. One minute I was happily under the custody of Mr. Sandman, and the next I had Tom under the covers with me squirming like a worm on a hook. He placed his face at point blank range to mine and started pouring oatmeal breath on me while jabbering between giggles, "Teevie! Teevie! Teevie! Hey, Bub!" He slipped in on the starboard-side of the bed and I got expelled on the port-side within about ten seconds. If they could market an alarm clock that effective, a fortune would be made overnight.

When it came to empathizing or showing tenderness, Tom was truly a master. In the presence of a baby, he would turn to mush. He'd study the infant as if this were the most precious thing he had ever laid eyes on and softly coo, barely touching its shoulder with a finger, and literally say, "Coo, Coo, Coo," as soft as the dew on a rose pedal. Babies picked up the message perfectly.

A favorite response of Tom's was, "I'm warm!" This was as much a greeting as it was a description that all was well in his world. When you asked how he was doing, he'd stop, look at you, smile, and say, "I'm warm." This short statement could easily have been a reference to the perfection of sitting on a square heat register on a frigid January morning.

CHAPTER 2

Outdoor Recreation

"Go outside and play,
Just be back by supper time."

—Mom

A motionless sack of potatoes. That sums up Tom's early attempts at swinging. He sat inertly on the swing seat. Physicists call it potential energy in that there was some possibility of movement, but not in the immediate future. Tom would sit patiently, hands wrapped around the chains, and wait for someone else's kinetic energy to power him. I would often be that source of propulsion. Giving him as big a push as possible, I then returned to my swing to resume trying to master the mechanics of pulling on my chains and pumping my legs. Tom's ride was never long lived, though, as his pendulum kept running low on energy and I'd have to go help him out again.

Tom was probably six and I four when we started on the swing set. It was now safely enclosed behind a wooden palisade-type fence (The Great Barrier) that Dad had recently erected for the express purpose of keeping Tom and me safe from our own wanderings. The swing set was located in the southeast corner of the exercise yard and a playground inmate could easily see between the four-foot high wooden pickets to freedom beyond. One could also see the outside world above the fence if one grabbed the cone shaped fence tops while standing on the lower rail of the fence. Or, one could even experience that freedom if, hypothetically, they got their other foot to the upper rail, pulled themselves up a little, and fell/vaulted over the spiked pickets. Razor-wire, more than likely, would have helped prevent many escapes and the eventual dismantling of this great civil engineering feat. It was reported that the first breakout occurred just two days after its completion.

Our swing set was your basic mid-century modern steel pipe, A-frame type unit, as opposed to the timber and composite color-coded contraptions that now populate most playgrounds. Today's swing sets are part of a safe, comprehensive "playground environmental experience" with slides, climbing apparatus, tunnels, nuclear reactors, and the like. Every opportunity for injury or harm has been carefully expunged with protective guard rails or padded materials. Not ours. Ours was the ubiquitous swing set of post-war American backyards: two A-frames on either end of a connecting pipe that established the height that the swing chains would attach at around seven feet, give or take a foot. Underneath the swing seats themselves, there was no cushy wood mulch or pea gravel, nor high-tech shredded rubber to cushion a fall. Nope. Below our swings were dished out patches of compacted earth with the compressive strength of concrete. Swinging was risky business.

Not many swing sets in 1950s America came with an instruction manual or a ponderous OSHA document itemizing potential health hazards and indicating safe operating techniques. I don't think they even came with the *Good*

Housekeeping Seal of Approval. I know ours did not. Ours was simple. You fall off the swing, you get hurt. You get a finger caught in the chain, you cut (or cut off) a finger. It was all very straight forward and everyone understood that a swing set was not a kid's toy. These were dangerous playground apparatus and children really shouldn't have been let near them, which is what drew us to them like moths to a porch light. For those of us who survived, they were great.

Our swings also had flat wooden seats with maybe sixteen inches of unobstructed butt space. That was enough so that you could even ride double with a second person on your lap facing you with their legs pumping on the back stroke. These were perfectly adequate seats. Sometimes they would be made out of plastic or hard rubber. These too were adequate. What was not an adequate seat was something that started creeping into playgrounds maybe in the late 1950s but definitely during the Cold War era. These were the U-shaped, sling-style, flexible seats that completely thwarted swingers in the free world. I know that this was, as trite as this may sound, part of a Communist conspiracy to frustrate young Americans and have them start questioning authority and be dissatisfied and disillusioned with wholesome American life. For heaven's sake, the sling smooched your butt cheeks together so hard that your legs had to pinch across each other, severely hampering your ability to pump, not to mention the weird, uncomfortable, half sideways seated position it left you in. You couldn't bail-out effectively, nor could you get any good distance on a jump. In short, sling seats ruined swinging. The decline of competitive swinging in the United States from that point on is really just academic.

Frustrations aside, there were three primary goals to swinging:

The first was to go as high as the sky. Nobody in our neighborhood really knew where the sky started, so this was a lofty goal indeed. You could say you made it, but really couldn't prove it. Now if you had blue scuff marks on your sneakers that would've been proof positive.

The second goal was a bit more definable, but alas, just as unattainable. That was to swing so hard as to wrap around the main support bar so that you would end up like a yoyo string wrapped around its spindle. We didn't really think this through completely, but it gave us incentive to pump the swing as hard as we could in hopes that we could get at least one good wrap. In all probability we might have made it to a position slightly beyond horizontal when gravity would work its limits on us. The chains would slack and the seat would stall out under us and we'd basically free-fall until the chains caught us before hitting the ground. This maneuver was risky, pushed the limits of the equipment, and usually caused a little minor whiplash. What's not to love?

The third goal was to swing hard enough to pull the swing set support legs out of the ground without actually toppling the swing set entirely. On many swing sets, the legs were just set in the earth. These were not much of a challenge. Dad, however, had poured a collar of concrete about a foot deep around each leg to permanently anchor the frame. This provided a pretty sizable challenge for which the neighbors (need I say, mostly boys) amply prepared. Sometimes it would take two of us, working collaboratively on the parallel swings, to contribute enough amplitude and angular momentum to yield a summation of forces greater than the restraining forces of the concrete ballast to get those suckers out of the ground. What a thrill to feel the swing set legs break free from earth's bonds just before you crashed to the ground with a hundred pounds of steel falling on top of you. This, of course, was advanced swinging.

But Tom just sat there. He tried pulling on the chains, but couldn't quite get the leg pump synchronized with the requisite weight shift to start the motion. He was the most patient student ever, however. Tommy didn't appear at all frustrated and seemed quite content just to idle in the permanent vertical position for long periods, fingers tightly gripped on the chain just in case spontaneous movement should occur.

This kind of arrested development, I learned, is typical of many persons with Down syndrome. With muscle tone weaker than a normal child's, and slower-to-develop coordination skills, many tasks that come quickly for normal children take extra time and practice for those with that extra twenty-first chromosome. The great news is that with practice (most Down's folks are very patient and enjoy repetition), they do succeed in achieving many of their goals. Abstract mental activities such as reading and math are usually one of the more difficult tasks to master, but most physical operations seem to eventually develop nicely. People with Down syndrome may ride bikes, play musical instruments, cook their meals, play sports, dance, hold meaningful jobs, and yes, even swing.

One day Tom got it. Divine inspiration perhaps? I don't know, but it clicked. At first it was just a wiggle and then an actual arc began to develop.

"Kick, Tom! KICK! Pull hard on the chains, Tom! YOU CAN DO IT!"

"Lean in, Tom. Watch me. Lean in—now kick hard—now lean back—now kick hard…"

He was flying. Tom was off the ground and picking up crucial altitude. Gears up, flaps retracted, he'd become a Melbourne Street pilot and the whole family couldn't have been prouder, especially me. I felt responsible for getting this recruit off the ground and pinning wings to his chest. Tom had a definite sense of his accomplishment and you could see a dignified pride that came over him when he started getting airborne. Finding ways to have Tom succeed was always rewarding for the whole family. It was like cheering for your favorite team, seeing them score, and knowing that they wouldn't have made it without your personal and timely involvement.

Tom went on to become a high performance swinger in the category of endurance. He was not into speed, height, nor bailing out, but he would swing for hours on end. He tested the outside limits of posterior nerve endings. He even spent hours flying those crappy, Soviet, sling-style seats. I think Tom was addicted to the near equivalent of perpetual motion that a good swing offered. For a little effort, you could get a wonderful rock with a slight weightless sensation on either end of the sweep. Once he had mastered the technique, Tom was known for staying in the seat for hours until someone told him to stop, or he heard the dinner bell.

When I was on the swing, I fantasized about flying; soaring, getting shot down, bailing out to safety, dodging machine gun fire as I made my way back to the base, then getting right back in the seat for another tour of duty. I don't know how much money I cost the U.S. government for wrecking so many airplanes, but it was substantial.

I wonder what Tom thought about while he swung. Maybe nothing, I suppose. Maybe he just enjoyed the moment for nothing more than a good swing; putting himself in neither the future nor the past, but staying in the transcendent now. I wonder how many times I have been absolutely content with the moment the moment it occurs. While I was out burning up kilocalories by the millions, Tom was quietly becoming a Zen swing master.

To the west side of the fenced-in area was the sandbox. Dad built a wooden structure about eight feet by six feet that contained a few cubic feet of finely crushed grains of gray gravel. Each spring, Dad took us to the local concrete ready-mix plant to pick up some fresh sand. He tossed a couple of galvanized bushel baskets into the Oldsmobile and we'd head over to Barny and Dickenson's Concrete

Sand and Gravel operations. Dad paid a nominal fee for a few shovels' full of sand to help replenish material that had gone AWOL over the previous year. Accompanying Dad to the ready-mix plant was always a highlight of the season. We'd drive up to this huge mountain of sand where we, the able bodied help, immediately started climbing this enormous man-made sand dune. It was huge, awesome, and intoxicating. Oh, to have this much play sand at our immediate disposal! However this sense of personal possession was not shared by the front-end loaders and conveyors taking sand out of the other side of the pile to make up concrete for the big ten yard mixer trucks. That would have been some shock to have a kid plop out of a ready-mix truck placing concrete at a construction site.

"Hey, wait a minute there, Bob, my job ticket didn't call for a 5% kid admixture! Send this load back."

While dad was busy shoveling and hefting the buckets back into the trunk, we'd start anticipating what this influx of new material was going to do to our sandbox back home. What extraordinary fun we'd have moving sand from one corner of the box to the other. Or, from one corner of the box to our pockets and eventually to all points indoors. When it got dumped into the sandbox it made wonderful hills and valleys and provided a great environment for our toy trucks and cars. We became masters of a gray, desert, flora-less world.

Pop quiz: If Father adds almost 300 pounds of sand each year to a sandbox to replace 300 pounds lost throughout the year, and if there are, on average, 150 active sandbox days per year, how much sand is in Mother's washing machine at the end of the year, assuming that one quarter of the lost sand is embedded in Tommy and Stevie's clothes when they come in from sandbox play?

Answer: About $75 worth. The cost to replace the bearings in the washing machine ruined by a heap of sand.

Tom, neighbors, and I spent a lot of time in this wonderful arena. Some of the other neighbors, however, were cats that found this sandbox to be the coliseum of litter boxes. It was the gold standard of feline restroom facilities. I recall finding these semi-rigid, sand coated Tootsie Rolls and believe I even tried to pretend to smoke one like a cigarette. I held it casually between my fingers as we had all learned how to do from ubiquitous cigarette ads that bombarded us in every medium and, of course, from the one out of every two adults (over fourteen) who smoked everywhere. "Cat turds taste good, like a cigarette should!"

Mom caught us being suave and sophisticated and then gave us a serious lecture on the dangers of feces and smoking (as well as smoking feces). Dad was then conscripted to build a wood and canvas canopy that could clamp down over the sandbox after Tom and Steve's excavating hours were over. This cat prevention system worked pretty well as long as some responsible person would lower the canopy at night. It got forgotten regularly, but Tom and I eventually learned to be alert regarding foreign objects before sitting in the sand to play. All in all we learned a good lesson in discernment. As cartoonist Scott Adams once noted, "Life is half delicious yogurt, half crap, and your job is to keep the plastic spoon in the yogurt."

The last major recreational opportunity in the incarcerates' exercise yard was the summertime presence of a flimsy inflatable swimming pool, located on the grass between the swing set and the sandbox. I remember Mom, verging on hyperventilation, inflating the pool one lung-full at a time. She'd then fill it with the garden hose while Jeff, Tom, and I watched in anticipation as the level of the water climbed. After an eternity, there might finally be eight inches of water just calling to our overheated little bodies. Mom cautioned us that the water needed to warm up a bit, but what did she know? Five minutes would certainly be enough to temper the fifty degree water. So in we'd go, and then having barely touched the water, out we'd fly. We'd study the situation, pensively looking at this Shangri-La that we couldn't yet enjoy (one of our many lessons in deferred gratification). After another five minutes, we'd regroup and make another assault. After twenty minutes of running through the pool, spilling half the water and giving the sun enough time to warm the remaining water to maybe sixty degrees, we'd settle into the pool, splashing like maniacs until the water was down to about one inch. At that point, usually without parental consent, someone would grab the garden hose and turn it on and start the refilling process. This was never as efficient as the initial fill as the discovery of a finger over the hose outlet meant that long range filling could occur with maybe a little collateral damage to whatever sibling was not holding onto the hose. Screaming and shouting echoed throughout the neighborhood.

As our parents began to realize that the great Melbourne Street Fence was not impenetrable, plans for part of its removal were considered. After only a couple of years, the south-side fence came down, opening the double-deep back yard and the nearby hillside for unimpeded exploration and carousing. A new chapter dawned.

After the "fall of the wall", I found that my expanded boundaries came with expanded responsibilities, or at least should have. Having, in essence, the entire world now open to me, I found new ways to try to injure or maim not only myself, but also other friends and neighbors. The so-called cognitive advantage I had over Tom was not manifested in all ways. Somehow back in the '50s, parents either didn't know or didn't care what happened to you during the day. It was best not to know all of the details unless you came back for lunch or dinner bloody or missing a limb. Pure stupidity was not considered reason enough for not sending you forth into the world to learn your own lessons. There were not as many lawyers then, so if you got hurt, it was your own fault—the way it should be. So, while Tom was safely, serenely, staying within now implied boundaries (contemplating the many great truths of life from a swing seat), I was out learning about applied physics, basic psychology, human anatomy, and feline psychosis. Some of those lessons included:

- A cape is not enough to enable me to fly off of the roof of the neighbor's chicken coop.
- The stick-like appendage attached to the steering column on my parents' car, when pulled down, can and will actually make the car go (regardless of the motor being on or not) if the car is parked on an incline. The car will also stop when there is an immovable object either in front of or behind the car.
- Five- and six-year-olds can do all sorts of stupid stuff, but when Dr. Steve and Nurse Jannie begin a practicum in Gross Anatomy and Gender Differentiation in the grove behind Jannie's grandma's house, Mom instantly develops x-ray vision. She can instantly see two little naked bodies through otherwise impenetrable earth, walls, and trees.
- While practicing a Sam Sneed tee shot with Dad's golf clubs, it is good to have a buddy not stand behind you, lest you learn what a double hit is and get acquainted with a new vocabulary word called "concussion."
- While playing back yard football, it is wise to note where the maple trees, cum goal posts, are located. This is especially important when catching a pass while looking in the opposite direction from which one is running.
- One cannot easily stop a homemade go-cart going down the Clayton Avenue Hill. Cars also use the street and it is a good idea to yield to them. Steering your go-cart into the ditch will eventually slow you down and even stop you. Repairs will be required. Splinters may need to be removed from embarrassing locations.

- Just because your fourteen-year-old brother is an electronic genius doesn't mean that he knows everything about electricity. Leaning against a nearby steel support column in the basement while touching a knob on one of his homebuilt radios will teach you (the shockee) the importance of grounding. A good laugh may be enjoyed by the other party (the shocker).

So, there in the backyard the split began. Two young sojourners started on their own inevitable divergent paths. I continued to build my high-risk resume of enlightenment regarding speed, flight, mechanics, construction, human sexuality, competition, and recreation, while Tom's path followed a slow curve of compliant dependency. The need for discourse, debate, and testing-to-failure, the hallmark of normal childhood discovery, was almost non-existent in Tom's world.

Unfortunately, much of Tom's passive dependency was a product of the times and the historic attitude that persons with mental disabilities were to be quietly tolerated and just left alone. These folks, after all, were basically "untrainable." That presupposition has been proven to be blatantly false for almost all but the most severe cases of Down syndrome. Slow does not equal none. Contemporary attitudes are remarkably different from that of the 1950s and '60s regarding what Down's people can do. Most reasonably sized communities offer many opportunities for the developmentally disabled to learn, work, and have exciting life experiences. It is fantastic! I was impressed when I read not long ago about a teenage woman with Down syndrome who learned to surf. Surf! Not only do you have to get over your fear of looking like a fool as you fall off and clamber back on a slippery surf board, but you also need to overcome the threat of getting hurt or drowning. I can't even screw up the moxie to think about learning to surf. It gives me the willies.

We are learning that there are many interventions, therapies, and programs that can unlock all kinds of opportunities for Down's folks of varying degrees of aptitude. It does require that we "regulars" create a different mind-set though, one that occasionally sets aside the modern paradigm of speed, efficiency, and convenience and modifies it with a little dose of the slow and repetitive. It is worth it.

CHAPTER 3

The Music Man

"He's a what?!
He's a what?!
He's a Music Man!"

—Meredith Wilson, "The Music Man"

As I progressed through the early years of kindergarten and grade school, Tom took a bit of a back seat in my life because I began to spend more time with kids in the neighborhood or my school class. Although not as regular a playmate, I can safely say that Tom was still always there for me when I needed him. I always knew where to find him when I had exhausted other playmates or distractions. If he wasn't outside (on the swing set or sandbox) then he might be in the sunroom sitting on a wooden rocking chair tuned into "Howdy Doody", "Captain Kangaroo", "Woody Woodpecker", maybe a soap opera, or something else on our tiny black and white TV screen.

Most likely though, Tom would be dancing to 78 rpm records on his little phonograph which he had mastered. Playing records on his own involved centering a seven inch diameter plastic disk on a 5/16 inch spindle while never bothering to turn the turntable off. The player was the standard rectangular box with three speeds. One could adjust the turntable to 16, 45 or 78 revolutions per minute and play records up to about twelve inches in diameter. We always found it amusing to put a 45 on and play it at 78, or put a 78 on and play it at 16. This was entertaining for at least a minute or two but was usually not appreciated by Tom. He would look us directly in the eye, which was always a little confusing given his crossed eye, and glower with an almost expressionless look. It said, "Who invited you to this party?" Up until the mid-1950s, all phonographs had real steel needles that followed the tracks in the vinyl. Occasionally, the needle would wear down to where it looked like a ball point pen tip and wouldn't follow the grooves of the record. This constituted a grave emergency. Mechanical failure for Tom was no different than for anyone else. I remember words of general complaint like, "No No Nooooo—Maaaake!" The rest of his mumbled expletives were in some sort of code none of us could translate.

"Somebody call tech support! We need a new needle in the tone-arm, STAT!"

Tom's records were short, wonderful ditties that recounted the tales of Superman, Popeye, Thumbelina, Pixie and Dixie, and a host of others in brash verse and even brasher music, all in about the lowest possible fidelity acceptable to the human ear. Each of Tom's records, of course, were marred with so many scratches that it was sometimes difficult to visually determine where the real grooves were. These scratches were not accidental, as each was carefully etched into the plastic surface by Tom's method of changing-out records. The technique was simple. While the turntable was rotating as fast as a scientific centrifuge, he would grab the tone-arm head from near the center of the record and drag it perpendicularly across the grooves. Each song ended with a fingernail-on-chalkboard screeching, "ZZZZZIIIIIIIPPPPPP" as the needle gouged out yet another unnecessary piece of plastic before the next record was loaded, or God forbid, the same record was queued-up to play all over again.

It is hard for me to imagine now that a whole industry was devoted to children's music and records. Able musicians, the cream of the crop from the Juilliard School of Music, must have written and performed each little jingle. I'm sure only the finest Oxford University English graduates wrote these pithy rhyming librettos. For young kids, these songs were probably okay, but for older people forced to listen there was significant collateral damage wrought on millions of brain cells. To call these tunes abhorrent is maybe too strong. However, I struggle to find a better term, so I guess I'll have to let others be the judge. Below is the libretto I've exhumed from the depths of my brain to "Popeye the Sailor Man."[8] These are not the cartoon show lyrics, but an original work by the Peter Pan Orchestra and Chorus—Peter Pan was the record label.

Instrumental intro (trombone and tuba):

> *Ba rum' pa-pa, Ba rum' pa-pa*
> *Ba rum' pa, rum' pa, rum' pa-pa*

Refrain:
> *"Popeye the sailor man,*
> *Eats his spinach from the can,*
> *There is no other stronger thaaaaan,*
> *Popeye the sailor man."*

Verse 1:
> *"He isn't very handsome*
>   *and he isn't very tall,*
> *But his heart's as big as big can be*
>   *with a love for one and all.*
> *Except when Bluto comes along*

just achin' for a fight.
Then Popeye eats his spinach
and knocks Bluto out of sight!"

Ba rum' pa-pa, Ba rum' pa-pa
Ba rum' pa, rum' pa, rum' pa-pa

Refrain:	"Popeye the sailor man,
Eats his spinach from the can,
There is no other stronger thaaaaan,
Popeye the sailor man."

Verse 2:	"If someone tries to come along
and bully Olive Oyl,
Popeye gets so fighting mad
his blood begins to boil.
He springs right into action
with the strength of fifty men.
The bully isn't apt to make
the same mistake again!"

Ba rum' pa-pa, Ba rum' pa-pa
Ba rum' pa, rum' pa, rum' pa-pa

Refrain:	"Popeye the sailor man,
Eats his spinach from the can,
There is no other stronger thaaaaan,
Popeye the sailor man."

Verse 2:	"He's got a friend named Wimpy
who dearly loves to eat.
The way he packs the food away
Is really quite a feat
Oh, Wimpey's always got a scheme
he's trying to pull off,
But all he ever seems to do

is eat more stroganoff!"
(I don't think the lyrics actually say "stro-
ganoff", but it certainly sounds like that.)

Ba rum' pa-pa, Ba rum' pa-pa
Ba rum' pa, rum' pa, rum' pa-pa

Refrain: *"Popeye the sailor man,*
Eats his spinach from the can,
There is no other stronger thaaaaan,
Popeye the sailor man."

Repeat refrain a thousand times in your head in the shower, during important business meetings, at church, while falling asleep, basically, whenever you don't want to hear it.

The songs were repetitive and annoying, similar to having to read redundant text. If you're like me, you skip the repetitive stuff as a way to tune-out, and that is exactly what we had to do to survive listening to Tom's repertoire. He would queue up some of these ditties maybe five to ten times a session.

This love of repetition is endemic in the Down's community. "Find something you like and stay with it" is the basic mantra. The fallout for the rest of us is that we must find and develop coping mechanisms to deal with these sometimes pesky vexations. Some might wear ear plugs, or simply remove themselves from the source of irritation. My favorite was to simply turn a deaf ear. It is a skill I honed with Tommy's music, but perfected over the years to the extent that I can be sitting right next to you, make eye contact, nod my head in agreement, and not hear a word you said because I'm off in another world. Ask my wife how good I am at this.

Unfortunately, I didn't completely tune-out as here I am remembering these lyrics pretty much by heart after over fifty-five years. It is testament that these records were played over and over and over again, and that these record companies were of the devil. It did not matter if you were actively listening to these tunes or not, the message seeped into every crevice of your brain. I know Satan was behind it all. These tunes so fully saturated your brain that once you started humming the melody, you might as well start making appointments with a counselor or an exorcist.

These demonic tunes are forever, parasitically anchored in my mind. I can go to bed at night hearing the little jingle in my head and earnestly pray that by morning my brain will be completely expunged of any vestige of "Popeye knocking Bluto out of sight." But, like a virus, it will still be there in the morning. Worse, an excerpt from "Superman"[9] will have taken its place.

> "From another planet
> Muscles made of granite.
> X-ray eyes and super brain.
> Is it a bird?
>   (Shouted) "NO!"
> Is it a plane?
>   (Shouted again) "NO!"
> What is it?"
> (Pregnant pause to really think about who it might be)
>   "It's ssssssSSSSSSSSSUUUUPER MAN!!!"

Now our children, when they were in the two to four year age range, just loved Tom's musical choices. They couldn't get enough of *Thumbelina*, *Mr. Ed*, *The Little Engine that Could*, or the immortal *Woody Woodpecker March*. I have to admit that I even had a friend from high school who would stop by when Tommy was visiting over Christmas to listen to his records with him. However, I am also not positively sure that this friend would have tested completely negative to the presence of tetrahydrocannabinol in his blood stream at the time, as he would tend to sing right along with the record.

> "It's ssssSSSSUUUUPER MAN.
> Who would guess that a reporter,
> Working for a daily paper,
> Hears about a case,
> Gets into his cape,
> Jumps into his boots,
> Changes into Superman."

Besides dancing and listening to his records, our kids were always amazed at his music filing and retrieval system. When asked for a specific title, Tom would, from only seeing the edge of the record in the case, carefully pluck it out of maybe sixty records. Magic? Maybe, but my theory is that Tom was really an incarnation of Superman himself. The circumstantial evidence is pretty weighty: 1) he was understated, 2) he wore glasses, 3) he gave the appearance of being a weakling, 4) if Lois Lane had lived in the neighborhood, she would have been fawning over him, 5) I think he owned a pair of Superman pajamas, and 6) no one, not a single solitary person, some even with pretty high IQ's (unlike the characters on the TV Superman show) ever suspected Tom to be the man of steel.

Tom loved music, and apparently this is almost a universal trait of Down syndrome people. Clinicians, family members, and care takers have almost categorically observed a strong connection between music and those with Down's. Some have postulated that persons affected with Down syndrome actually have superior musical proclivities over normally developing children of the same mental age.[10] This conclusion is probably a bit exaggerated, but several studies have concluded that their musical ability is at least on par with young normal kids.[11]

It has been demonstrated that Down's persons can play musical instruments, sing, and dialog with other musicians in improvisational settings. Although reading musical notation is difficult, other means of teaching have been found to assist in learning the proficiency of an instrument as well as the accurate replication of songs.[12] Many have a finely tuned ear and can exactly repeat a rhythmic phrase or song upon hearing it only once. It seems that music offers some wonderful avenues of expression for a large segment of this population.

Although Tom had a great fondness and appreciation for music, it did not bleed over into his performance sector. Tom's limited speech capacity didn't help but also he couldn't carry a tune. Rhythmically, he stunk!

Tom danced to almost all music. His personal rhythm and the meter of the song never really matched. It did not matter. Tom simply rocked sideways from one foot to the other wearing the carpet out where each determined foot landed a couple of thousand times a day. He was never opposed to dancing partners, per se, but clearly his choreographer designed his dances for one person. Also, he would outlast any normal dance partner. Much like his swinging, endurance was his gift. Powered by some outside nuclear force, he would have left the Energizer Bunny merely twitching by noon. How the arches of his feet survived this daily regimen for fifty-odd years remains one of the great mysteries of our time. Other than a secret stash of kryptonite, I don't know how he persevered for hours at a time, rocking back and forth.

In the early 1960s, Tom's personal phonograph was replaced with a new, cheap plastic Dejay brand Special Edition record player. This thing was so flimsy, I don't know how it survived the type of abuse Tom heaped on it. My mother still keeps this record player in working condition and has his complete 78 collection housed in one of those flimsy cardboard 45 record cases that have a hinged top and a plastic handle. I'm not sure there is a market for children's records of the 1950s and '60s, but should there be, I know of a pretty good stash in near mint condition.

The record playing and listening in the house was not done on low fidelity record players, though. No indeed! In about 1958 or '59, Dad purchased a technologically advanced, 33 1/3 RPM (LP), stereophonic, automatic record changing console with a remote speaker cabinet to allow two channels of music pleasure to come at you (if you really thought about it hard enough). This machine had lots of knobs that we were instructed not to touch. These dealt with things like bass and treble modifications, RPM selection, and the all-important speaker balance knob, which helped render a somewhat stereophonic experience if you sat in the right spot and really concentrated. Naturally there was a volume control knob. The tone arm was rather light and had a diamond stylus instead of a needle. We were not allowed to touch The Stereo as kids. We had to handle the records by the edges, lest a microscopic mark from our finger-print would derail the sensitive needle, I mean stylus. Jeff ignored the edict almost immediately and within six months, I was fooling with all of the knobs. One could put a stack of up to five records on the automatic spindle and play them one after the other, just like that. After about three records though, the weight on the turntable began to slow the speed down just a little and you could get some interesting sounds coming out of the speakers after five or more records were piled up.

I believe Tom was the only sibling who obeyed the edict not to mess with the stereo. When a long play record needed to be changed, he waited for Mom to do the work. She queued up a couple of platters, hit the start button and then went about doing what moms did. Tom listened and danced to marches (what Tom called "Soosa," shorthand for John Philip Sousa), show tunes, musicals, and Lawrence Welk (everyone listened to Welk in 1959). These all came from my parents' growing stereo record collection. Although he wasn't allowed to touch the tone arm and ZZZZIIIIPPP it across the record, his dancing still did significant damage to the fidelity of sound. With each footfall, his incessant two-step inflicted divots and pits into each vinyl disk. You can still hear the remnants of each thudding foot and the associated bouncing of the tone arm and the regular "dip, dip, dip" coming out of the big speakers. This is all a part of Tom's recorded history marking his march to the beat of a different drummer.

Band concerts in the park were another special part of Tom's music world in the summertime. In Ames, Iowa, where Mom, Dad, and Tom resided since 1984, there is a downtown city park known as Band Shell Park. Each Thursday from June through July, the Ames Municipal Band puts on an hour long concert outside. It is a wonderful American tradition carried over from the nineteenth century, which is still practiced in a lot of Midwest towns and villages. The musicians are all volunteers, so the quality of the music can vary quite a bit, but it really doesn't matter. It's just a great way to take a little respite from the weekly grind and see a few of your neighbors. Now tell me, who doesn't like the idea of taking an hour off every week in the summer to spend a balmy evening on the lawn, scarfing down a bag of popcorn with five hundred of your closest friends listening to John Philip Sousa or Karl King marches? If it doesn't conjure up nostalgic images of Meredith Wilson's "The Music Man", I don't know what else can.

At eight o'clock sharp, the emcee takes his position and introduces the maestro and the members of the, "Aaaaaaaames Municipallllll Baaaand!" A rousing rendition of the national anthem kicks off the concert, where it is uncommon for people not to sing along with the featured soloist. About ten rows of folding lawn chairs back, amidst fireflies and other folks on blankets, Dad, Mom, and Tom would sit. Tom wore a ball cap, cradled a couple of magazines on his lap, held a candy bar in one hand, and a Coke in the other. Some people prepare for final exams, Tom prepared for Thursday night band concerts.

Thursday night was a sacramental religious experience for Tom. There were few exceptions to his participating in this weekly event. I'm not sure how he kept track of the days of the week, but he somehow always knew that Thursday's were band concert night. If a particular piece really moved him, he'd start excitedly applauding well before the music finished (always careful to set his soft drink and candy bar down first). On occasion he'd spontaneously jump out of his lawn chair and start dancing.

Should a favorite march be announced, like Meredith Wilson's "Seventy-six Trombones," and before the director had a chance to even drop his baton, Tom would stand and shout, "Oh boy! Oh boy! Oh boy!" Unmolested by societal norms and expectations, and in his understated way, Tom's body language would say, "Don't you people get it? This is, 'Seventy-six Trombones', for heaven's sake!"

When Tom was hospitalized a few years ago with a severe respiratory ailment and not making much progress, I made up a few cassette tapes of some of his favorite songs. I like to think that being able to listen to a John Philip Sousa march or a few show tunes helped him along in his healing process. My theory was that there was no way he could die listening to "Semper Fidelis" pulsing through his head, and I was right.

I have to give my mom a lot of credit for not only enduring years of Tom's endless cycle of the same old music but also encouraging what musical abilities he had. I'm not sure Mom had ever read or heard anything about Down syndrome folks and their innate love of music, but she must have sensed that Tom could express himself through music better than any other form of communication. She gave him musical carte blanche for his entire life.

CHAPTER 4

Mannerisms

"Everybody's normal 'til you get to know them."

—John Ortberg

Idiosyncratic is the word that comes to mind. Tom was his own man and not afraid to show it in public. He had many mannerisms that set him apart and was unapologetic about them. Sometimes they were embarrassing to other members of the family, but it did not usually alter his behavior, nor matter one hoot to him. All were benign and some downright endearing. A couple of his habits come to mind.

The Art of Dangling

One of the earliest mannerisms that I remember was the cloth dangling. I don't think I have ever seen anyone else with such a deep concern for the folds created when dangling a washcloth or dish towel. Dangling was quite simple and I remember trying it a few times (mostly just social dangling—I never really got the same buzz that Tom obviously got, and I never inhaled).

Dangling consisted of gently holding a towel by opposite corners and then slowly raising one corner above the other, dropping the other corner coincident with the rise of the first. All very methodical and intentional. Then repeated a thousand times. There was a hypnotic affect imparted, I'm sure, as Tom fell into a cathartic trance watching new folds being created and then dissipate. It must have been like having your own portable ocean to gaze upon with waves forming then crashing against the shoreline, or like watching a flag in a gentle breeze wiggle and writhe with almost anthropomorphic gestures. Tom studied these folds as if he was studying for the bar exam. Concentrated, reverenced eyes took in each subtle move as it appeared, then disappeared, with another ripple being formed right behind the last. Each moment as precious as the next. Even though this was a silent activity, it could grow annoying being in the same room with Tom and towel for an hour or more.

"Tom, stop the dangling!"

Tom also dangled Slinkys. I don't know who created the Slinky, but whoever it was made a pile of money and they should also be put in prison for life. Talk about bilking the public! It makes Bernie Madoff look like a Boy Scout! Somehow, someone in Slinky-Land marketing convinced the entire world that they were fun and educational and that every kid born in the last half of the twentieth century needed one. I don't know what part of fun they were talking about except that you could shoot these things at targets (like your kid sister—"Mom, Steve's shooting his Slinky at me!") and they would supposedly recoil right back to you like a boomerang. Well, they sort of recoiled, but usually they ended up as a mass of coiled metal snarled into a hopeless nest of gnarly, knotted curlicues. Oh yeah, you could also walk them down a set of stairs. A genius might end up with the Slinky at the bottom—maybe. My personal record is three steps. It usually got abandoned on the stair for an unsuspecting family member to find while carrying a load of laundry to the basement.

Okay, I do have to confess that Slinky's were also educational. Really. I remember studying wave theory in high school physics with a Slinky and writing a lab report on the relationship between amplitude and frequency (or maybe something to do with wavelength). We paired off in teams with a stretched-out Slinky between us resting on the terrazzo floor. Then we'd start imparting a force on the Slinky and get a half-wave, then a complete wave then we found the first harmonic, and then we'd start shooting them at the team next to us, hopelessly snarling the Slinky for the next period's class.

Anyway, while the rest of us were trying to get these coils of metal to walk down the steps, figure out what the heck an amplitude was, or more likely, trying to get one untangled, Tom was busy schleeeenking his between one hand and the other. It never snarled for him because he was way to gentle with it. He treated his Slinky with the dignity and respect that it probably didn't deserve. Tom tended to be the gentlest person on the planet not only with things, but also with people (he would have been a terrible politician). It was a Zen kind of thing for Tom— the hypnotic visual appeal as the Slinky coils caught the reflected light, moving back and forth, back and forth. Schleeeenk—schleeeenk—schleeeenk.

"Tom! Go back to your towel!"

The towel or Slinky was his primary pacifier. How we pacify ourselves is an interesting phenomenon. I've mildly made fun of Tom and this repetitive habit and, by association, the similar repetitive traits that many Down's people have. However, before I get too sanctimonious, I think the rest of us need to be reminded that we are also not far removed from this behavior.

People have even made some real money off of our apparent need to calm ourselves with toys that do almost nothing but make a repetitive noise or motion. Before I condescendingly laugh too loudly at others' foibles, I am reminded of yoyos, desk clackers, and those insane wooden paddles with the rubber ball tethered by a two foot long elastic band. I really need not mention other pacifiers that we "normal" people may employ that tend to kill us like cigarettes, alcohol, and drugs.

Magazines

To my knowledge, Tom did not read. If he did he fooled a lot of people. Maybe at break time, down at the house where he lived for twenty-five years, some of the residents got together and talked about the meaning of *The Brothers Karamazov*, but I just can't see it. To my knowledge, Tom didn't write either. I don't think he grasped the symbolic representation present in a single English character, let alone figure out the entire alphabet (the letter T in the American Sign Language lexicon excepted). There is no evidence that he recognized his name in print or could write it. Literacy was not his thing.

Tom could make marks, though, or color in a coloring book. I think it was about people like Jackson Pollock and my brother that the adage about coloring outside of the lines came about. Tom was adamant that his artistic voice would not be confined. A coloring book page was meant to be filled, despite those pesky pre-printed pictures of bourgeois, cartoon animals with the big eyes. He colored vigorously with whatever you stuck in his hands and made bold marks that resembled rain falling at a thirty degree angle. Stunning expressions of self-actualization? Maybe, but regrettably, nothing that ever showed up in the *New Yorker* magazine.

Tom loved printed material. He especially liked magazines and he internalized their contents like no one before or after. Hoarding paper is sometimes a compulsion of persons with Down syndrome and this habit had a certain resonance with Tom. He collected magazines from around the house by the hundreds. If there was a magazine somewhere, anywhere, he sniffed it out. He would have found magazines under my bed mattress if there had been any there, so there weren't. Honest! You would see Tom moving about the house with a growing armful of current literature (including electrical engineering trade journals of Dad's). Compulsive episodes of magazine collecting were seek and destroy missions. Mostly his collection was the standard fare that Mom would pick up at the grocery store or were sent to our home. Normally we had a pretty good supply of *Woman's Day, Better Homes and Gardens, Time, Newsweek, Life, Look, National Geographic, Boys Life,* and the like. After a hefty load of magazines were found, Tom plopped in the middle of the living room and opened each one to a specific page while he carefully placed it in front of him. He created these radiating concentric semi-circles of printed material with him sitting at the epicenter of it all. Twenty, thirty, maybe fifty magazines would bow down to him. There he sat, cross legged, Buddha-esque, and beaming with contentedness. Each magazine was carefully picked up one at a time, caressed with his eyes, and then ceremoniously replaced exactly from where it had been taken.

The content of what he looked at varied and raised questions in the family's mind as to what was going on through his. He was intrigued and sometimes troubled about any picture that had a person bound or even with their hands placed benignly behind their back (pictures of Prince Charles comes to mind). War pictures also seemed to crop up regularly. These were disturbing issues to Tom and he wanted them to be present in his ink menagerie. He also liked looking at pictures with girls or comely women. If there was an ad for, say, Maidenform bras in one of the magazines, you can guess to which page that *Woman's Day* would be opened. Who knows, I might have even interrupted my busy schedule for a quick gander at some of his more daring selections.

Tom created these living papyrus assemblages and they grew as he found yet more journals around the house until his montage took on a life of its own and became a major contribution to urban blight, not to mention a tripping hazard. Mom, being much more averse to clutter than say, me, would finally swoop in, collect the mags, and redistribute them to either their proper end table or the garbage bin.

Tom's word for any printed material was, "bookbookbookmagazine," even though he never reached for a bound book that I can recall. This unquenchable lust for printed material persisted his entire life and compelled him to great lengths to obtain more. While living at his group home a few years back, my folks got a frantic phone call from the house steward stating that Tom was missing. He had somehow quietly slipped out of his home and had gone wandering.

This was a serious matter. The home he shared with four or five others was only a driveway's length away from US Route 69 and fifty-five mile per hour traffic. The search was frantically proceeding when a phone call from a neighbor (who happened to live on the other side of the highway) came in and she said she thought someone from Tom's house was in her house. Everyone took a deep sigh of relief. Apparently, while the neighbor had been out running errands, Tom had broken in. He probably just turned a door knob on an unlocked door and walked in, as breaking anything was always considered bad form for Tom. When the lady of the house returned, to her amazement, she found our literary critic sitting cross-legged on the floor of her kitchen, surrounded by concentric semi-circles of magazines that he had accumulated from his newly discovered lending library. Along with the journals, there was also a half-gallon of ice cream (nearly emptied of its contents) sitting between his legs. The well sated perpetrator was identified and escorted back to his residence. The guilty party muttered, scolding himself with his characteristic self-effacing "No! No! No!" all the way back.

Measures were taken to ensure that did not happen again. After a little careful observation by house staff, they were able to figure out a little cause and effect. Apparently, Tom kept a pretty keen lookout for the Postal Service every day and knew about when they fed the mail box at the end of the driveway. After the postman would leave, and when no one was looking, he'd let himself out and go check the mailbox for any magazines.

"No magazines in this box. Maybe there might be some in those other mailboxes so nicely lined up on the opposite side of the highway."

The staff decided to try a little behavior modification by installing an unofficial mailbox, attached to the group-home house itself, expressly for Tom. Then they would go about making sure there was a recycled magazine to stuff in his mail box every day so that Tom would have a treasure to find on his side of the block. A little creative thinking on the staff's part stopped the forays across the highway and probably helped keep Tom's life-span from becoming significantly shortened.

Magazines also made wonderful gifts for lazy brothers. Christmas presents for Tom were always a snap. I'd go down to the public library where they had a magazine swap for second-hand journals. I'd scoop up a dozen mags and head out, roll them up, throw a little wrapping paper on 'em, and behold, a treasure. He'd squeal with joy that once again I had given him used magazines for a Christmas gift.

Sometimes I felt pretty cheap, but what do you give a man who has everything?

Bean ball

Games with balls were always a hit with Tom. He was an avid baseball fan and watched as many games on TV as he could. You'd ask him who was playing and it was always the same: "Yankees!" Both teams were the Yankees. Baseball equaled Yankees. My little league team, "Red Barn" (for our sponsors, the Red Barn Supper Club) were, the Yankees. "Mickey Mantle," likewise, was the quintessential baseball player. No matter who was at bat, it was always Mickey Mantle. There was also only one announcer and that was Pee Wee. Pee Wee Reese, the great hall of fame shortstop for the Brooklyn (later LA) Dodgers through the 1940s and '50s. Following his active baseball career, Pee Wee went into announcing games for CBS. Along with Dizzy Dean, the duo would fill in all of the chatter necessary to not only follow the game but also anything else that popped into their heads while trying to keep a TV audience interested in a game that is really meant to be enjoyed in person, outside, at the ball park. Dizzy and Pee Wee were both Tom's friends, but somehow it was usually just Pee Wee that Tom could pronounce easiest, so he got adopted into our family on Saturday afternoons during baseball season, his voice incessantly babbling on like a cheerful mountain stream.

Tom was not to be entirely trusted with balls, though, as he had a tendency to misuse the privilege inherent in good sportsmanship. Most of our ball games consisted of rolling a big red rubber playground ball back and forth between us. Sometimes our sister Nancy might join us in the living room and we'd all sit about ten feet away from each other, legs splayed apart, and roll the ball at each other. This proved entertaining for a minute or two. Then we'd start to bounce the ball at each other. This progressed to standing and trying to have Tom catch the ball. This was more like trying to throw an egg back up into a nest from which it had fallen. Tom's reflexes were a little slow so you had to have him hold his arms out, kind of close together, elbows bent, and then carefully aim and gently toss the ball and hope he'd hold on before it dribbled to the floor. Catching was not his forte. We would continue with our underhand tossing until someone stopped paying attention or some-one else walked into the room. If you turned your back to Tom, you were a marked person. It was then that he would demonstrate his classic overhand changeup. He'd rear back, and before anyone could be warned, the rubber ball would be launched at someone's head with unerring accuracy. A baseball would have really hurt. In terms of violent actions, this was Tom's equivalent of being bad-to-the-bone. He'd usually squeal with delight, then reprimand himself with the incriminating, "No! No! No!" Guilt never looked so fun.

Church Participation

Tom never missed a chance to go to church. Granted, some of those occasions were compulsory, but even if they were dictated by the authorities, he didn't seem to mind. He loved to go and sit quietly on a hard pew with the family and participate as much as he could—standing, sitting, sitting cross legged. He seemed to be as content as one could be just being in the sanctuary soaking up the ambi-ance of the place. Some people seem to draw deep refresh-ment from the mountains or a quiet lake, maybe a sail on the ocean or a ride on a horse. Tom seemed to draw that kind of rejuvenation and satisfaction from being in what some may term a sacred place. I think it was holy for Tom and he liked it. It is pure conjecture on my part, but I believe he was tuned into a different channel than most of us. I think that there was some spirit-talk going on regularly between Tom and his creator that I have only occasionally tasted.

When a congregational hymn was sung, he would dutifully pull one of the hymnals from the pew-back rack, open it randomly, and place it, oftentimes upside down (it didn't really matter), on his stomach. Tom had enough of a stomach ledge that there was little chance of the hymn book sliding off. He'd sit there, cross-legged in the pew, unless Mom quietly said to "Put 'em (your legs) down." Then, as the rest of the congregation would sing, he'd silently jabber along, lips moving to a different tune perhaps, as his hands would hold the red book in place. The singing would end and the hymnal would go back into the rack. If you can't read, if you can't sing, if you don't know the words, use osmosis to suck out the juice.

My parents regularly picked Tom up so that he could attend Sunday morning services at the United Methodist Church. Tom thoroughly enjoyed getting dressed up for the occasion. He'd let Dad tie his necktie and he'd even resist the urge to tuck his pant legs into his socks. He loved the music, the space, and the donuts and coffee served in the fellowship hall afterwards. On Sundays that he wasn't able to attend, you had better at least have saved a donut and wrapped it in a napkin for later consumption. If not, you were subject to a torturous inquisition of "Donutcoffee— eat,eat,eat donut-coffee." This grueling banter would be incessant and unrelenting until you were compelled to stop by the Dunkin' Donuts for a glazed raised and a cup of coffee.

Learning to live with Tom and his idiosyncrasies was like learning to live with, well, anyone. Most of Tom's manners were benign and to get him to stop or modify an annoying behavior, all you had to do was ask. It was actually quite refreshing. You asked and he dutifully responded. It required no passive aggressive build-up nor stormy demonstration that frequently happens between us "normals" as we try to modify each other's behavior. Tom never left in a huff after calmly putting his towel down.

CHAPTER 5

Sports

"It's one, two, three strikes
You're out!
At the old ballgame."
——Edward Meeker ("Take Me Out to the Ballgame")

The surname Prater and the word sports are not synony-mous, at least in my branch of the family. I'm sure there are tons of Praters down south, where we're a dime a dozen, that are football heroes and basketball stars, complete with cheerleaders on each arm. My immediate family though is not that athletic. It's not because we didn't try or weren't interested. It's probably because we lacked that competi-tive killer instinct, along with the fact that we were all twigs growing up. My oldest brother Jeff and I are both six foot four and we were that tall in about ninth grade. One may think that is not so bad until you consider we were only 135 pounds until we were twenty-five years old. We would have been snapped like a dry stick under an elephants' foot if we had gone out for tackle football or some other contact sport. Luckily (most probably unluckily), the underweight issue has since abated.

In other words, we were destined to be "in the band." It was a huge disappointment to realize that we would never make that diving catch with time running out to win the big game and alas, never be idolized by all the beautiful girls in high school. On the other hand, it was a huge revelation to me when I was a junior in high school that the band (and choir) were chock full of beautiful girls whom I got to sit next to and talk to and get to know and maybe even date. Not only that, but I still have two (count 'em) original equipment, working knees and no debilitating head injuries.

To their credit, Mom and Dad taught us to play a respectable game of tennis. One year I even played for the high school team, but I was not that good in a competitive setting. I had parts of my game that came together and sparkled, only to have the rest come crashing down. I choked a lot when the pressure rose. One of the guys on the team decided that my nickname would be "Ichabod", as in Ichabod Crane in Washington Irving's short story *Sleepy Hollow*. The moniker stuck, not just because I was tall and gangly, but also because the name usually got shortened to, "Ickky", which pretty much summed up my tennis career.

After our family moved to another town following that spring foray into tennis, I tried out for basketball and actually made their junior varsity team. I was not called Ichabod at my new school, but I could have been. Despite being the tallest one on the squad, I scored the fewest points and finally realized that in order to play this game, I needed to know how to run, jump, dribble and, oh yes, shoot the ball through an incredibly small hole ten feet above the floor. I learned how to ride the pine on the Horace Greeley High School bench, and I got included on a nice team picture for our school yearbook (I'm listed as N. Nelson on page 96). As an aside, it didn't help that our school mascot was a "Quaker" (as in William Penn, the guy on the oatmeal box). So while the opposing teams' cheerleaders were pertly bouncing around in their short pleated skirts leading cheers like, "Punch 'em, Crunch 'em, Grind 'em up and Munch 'em" our primly attired cheerleaders, in bonnets and ankle length black dresses, encouraged our team with chants like, "Don't Hurt Thy Adversaries, Quakers!" or, "Let Thy Opponents Shoot in Peace, Quakers!" It was hard to get truly aggressive when your school mascot is named after historic pacifists.

Aside from my one year as a little league pitcher with the Red Barn Supper Club, that was about it for organized sports in our immediate Prater family. My brother, Dr. Jeffrey Prater, who is a noted musical composer, university professor, author, Fulbright Scholar, multi-lingual, and smart-as-a-whip, still suffers from serious sports inferiority complex syndrome from failing to make a little league team when he was ten. Competition was tough in Vestal, New York, and the little league officials wanted kids to find out early in life if they were or were not cut out for good ol' American, go-for-the-throat, take-no-prisoner kind of athletics. Jeff didn't make the cut, so he and his Harvey Kuene signature ball glove were sent packing after the first day of try-outs.

"Sorry kid, go find yourself a nice clarinet and a band to blow it in."

Not to toot my horn too loudly, nor make my brother feel any worse, but I still have the elegant trophy for being on the team that won the minor league championship of the Vestal Little League in 1962. It's a beautiful trophy too, in a post-depression era kind of way. I'll describe it. It is a baseball (with my name written on it in faded ball-point pen) glued to a two inch by two inch by three inch high block of wood attached with a couple of nails to an almost square sturdy base of quarter inch plywood. On one side of the triumphal column the noted achievement is typed on a tiny slip of paper and slid behind a piece of thin plastic, which is anchored to the vertical post with what looks like number 4 finishing brads. Despite the fact that the glue holding the ball to the top of the trophy shaft is smeared to high heavens, the type written text is not even close to horizontal, and the protective plastic overlay (nailed over the text) is not centered, it is still a coveted remembrance of my achievements and glory as an American athlete.

In all fairness to my brother, I should report that the following year, after my celebrated success as a minor league starting pitcher, when I tried out for the major league Little League teams, alas, I too failed and was sent shuffling back home, limp glove hung over the end of my bat as it rested on a dejected shoulder like a hobo's bandana bindle. If there was anything sorrier than a kid rejected from playing Little League baseball, I can't think of what it might be.

"What kind of an American am I, anyway? Maybe I should be deported to Russia!"

I would not pick up a ball and glove and stride out onto a ball diamond again for almost twenty years. It wasn't until I was recruited to our architecture studio's softball team in graduate school at the University of Minnesota. Here, finally, the desperate healing needed after two decades of abject rejection could take place. The main thing that made this such a cathartic, memorable experience was that I could run the base path (presuming I got a hit) with a can of beer in my hand. Over the years, I have forgotten exactly what our record was, but I think it was pretty good. Three cases a game seems to come to mind.

That was the sad story of the Prater sports legacy until a day in 1985 when the sports gods finally smiled down on us with the discovery of the latent talent of Tom "Head-Pin" Prater at the Century Bowling Lanes. Apparently, Tom's slow, methodical approach to just about everything was an incredible asset to a game where speed means nothing (almost nothing) and accuracy means everything (almost everything). Bowling was a perfect match.

He and his housemates bowled every Tuesday afternoon and Tom was there, sporting his own eight pound ball and personalized bowling shoes. No fungus infected rental shoes for this pin-splitter. No sir-ree Bob! After perfecting the two-handed, between-your-legs roll, he went on to employ a power roll that actually used his fingers in the pre-drilled holes. Standing at, or on, or maybe beyond, the foul line with his legs shoulder width (or wider) apart, he got into what we sports aficionados call "The Zone." Tuning out all distractions, he stared down the alley about five feet from his feet, and approximately where the ball landed after it left his hand. Then, Tom swung the ball between his legs, aiming at something three lanes to his right. After enough momentum had been established (three or four swings), he would straighten out the last swing and let 'er fly.

Thump.

The ball would dent the alley a few feet away from him and begin the slowest roll recorded in the annals of bowling history. Only the second coming of Christ has taken longer. A person could run errands and still get back in plenty of time to see the least violent collision between ball and pin that ever occurred. The only one patiently waiting would be Tom, hands folded behind his back, standing lump-stock still and occasionally glancing up to watch the ball trace a line exactly down the middle of the lane. Then, in super slow motion, things would happen. A pin would fall, then another, and another. After a minute or so, when the air would clear of loose flying splinters, you'd notice that he'd taken out nine of ten pins. All of that damage done by a ball that, if it had been moving less, would have been sitting in a lawn chair finishing off a frozen Margarita! As a matter of fact, often the ball would stop on the lane, leaning up against a towering pin like an unlikely couple waiting to go out on a date.

Meanwhile, Tom would still be at the foul line, hands clasped behind his back, waiting quietly for something more to happen.

Thud.

The final pin would decide to drop, even though the ball had technically come to a halt thirty seconds earlier. The gallery, of course, would erupt with cheers and Tom would be told to sit down. While the next bowler was getting ready, one of the alley attendants would trot down the lane and kick the ball over the edge to restart the pin setting cycle, which had fallen asleep during this whole episode.

To be honest, Tom had his fair share of splits, but to our amazement, he often rolled a couple of strikes and picked up a spare or two during a game to end up with a score of 120 or so. It was always fun and fulfilling to watch the testosterone-laden high school kids on the next alley over hurling their flame balls, (the ones that never touch the wood floor), only getting scores of 110.

Tom also excelled at bocce ball, which is a game where a small ball is rolled out and then contestants roll balls toward it with the objective of being closest to the target. The nice thing for Tom in this sport was that the ball didn't need to knock anything over. The nasty violence of balls slamming into pins was totally absent. One might hear an occasional click as one ball kissed another, but that was the worst of it.

Tom played in several Special Olympics as well as other tournaments and ended up collecting quite a few trophies, medals, and ribbons for bowling, bocce ball, and softball throw. Our children, when they were in grade school, were amazed at the amount of hardware Uncle Tom had in his bedroom commemorating his prowess at these contests.

"How can Tommy be so good?" they'd ask. "How come he has so many trophies and medals?"

Then of course, I'd proudly show them my Little League trophy along with a couple of certificates of participation. I'm not certain, but I think they might have been slightly impressed with their father.

CHAPTER 6

Off to State

"Our team is out there
Out there to fight.
We like their courage,
We like their might…"

Football rouser

Usually when we hear the phrase "off to state," we think of our high school football or basketball team heading to a championship game or our best musical students getting invited to play a massive concert with the finest high school musicians from around the state. Sometimes, it conjures up thoughts about leaving the safety and security of our home to hone our skills and try our luck at the Big State University, hoping to find and develop aptitudes that will give us satisfaction and gainful employment for the next forty years.

When Tom went off to state, it was none of the above. Tom's state did not promise him anything other than survival and perhaps a chance to learn a few additional personal skills. Tom's state was known as Rome State School for the Mentally Retarded. Founded in 1893, it was originally known as The New York State Asylum for Unteachable Idiots. That probably wouldn't have looked good on a resume´.

By the early twentieth century, attitudes and perceptions regarding people with intellectual disabilities had become more humane than the 1800s. Nevertheless, conventional wisdom in America held to the notion that these members of our society should be removed from our everyday lives and sequestered (out of sight, out of mind). Heaven forbid that we should come in contact with them or know to whom they belonged.

In the early 1960s, at the time of Tom's admission to Rome State, his school and similar state institutions were still classified as asylums and their residents as inmates. When Tom resided there, the large sign from the main road could have easily read, "Rome State School for the Mentally Retarded and the Mentally Ill," as all five thousand inmates shared the same campus. There was often little distinction made between the mentally retarded and the mentally ill. There is a significant difference.

Prior to Tom's move to Rome State School, valiant attempts were made by Mom and Dad to provide educational and enriching experiences for him. They were active members in the local fledgling chapter of the Association for Retarded Children (ARC),** which was growing in strength and numbers across the country in the early 1950s. The Triple Cities chapter was able to pool resources

---

** The term "retarded" has taken on such a demeaning connotation that this organization dropped any reference to it in their name in 1992. Instead of being an acronym for Association of Retarded Children (then Citizen), its name became simply, "The ARC." On their web page they state that the "r" stands for "respect."

and fund one teacher for a small private school for local children with developmental disabilities. ARC even bought a couple of station wagons and rotated responsibilities for transporting their children to and from the small classroom space located above a local business in downtown Endicott. I remember tagging along with Tom on days when it was Mom's turn to drive.

Then, in the latter 1950s, public schools in New York were mandated to provide special needs education. Tom and several other children from the Triple Cities area consequently attended these special classes at an area public school and were what might be loosely called "mainstreamed." This wasn't quite the case, as these kids were segregated and in their own classroom with a special education teacher for the day. Interaction with normal students was almost nonexistent other than slight incidental contact. Eventually, Tom's learning potential was deemed too low to qualify for publicly offered educational services. Other higher achieving children were admitted to the often overcrowded and under-budgeted classrooms. Eliminated from the program, with no place outside the home to receive enriching experiences and educational services, Tom was now back at home again all day—dangling cloths, listening to records, and watching TV.

Jeff was thirteen, Tom was eleven, I was nine, and Nancy six. We were all in school at the time. Mom and Dad were caught between the proverbial rock and a hard place. How could they adequately help three children when so much custodial time must be spent caring for Tommy? Dad traveled quite a bit for IBM, which was expanding exponentially in that era, and he'd be gone on a business trip maybe every five or six weeks. Our closest relatives were a thousand miles away in Iowa, so there wasn't any regular help to be expected from them.

Our folks were stretched increasingly thin with Jeff, Nancy, and me at critical development stages. I think they felt they could not adequately attend to both our needs and Tom's. I know that I struggled in school. My reading skills were behind the class norm and I attended remedial reading classes through junior high, when the school stopped offering such classes. Nancy, in second grade, was probably a better reader than I was in sixth. I also had other interests (like football and messing around with friends) that often took precedence over studies. My study habits probably could have been better monitored if our parents had had a little more discretionary time. I also knew how to effectively avoid my studies and disappear by hiding in Jeff's shadow, who I thought was the smartest person ever. He knew how to build radios and even had an amateur ham radio license when he was twelve. He taught me Morse code and everything. I can even remember his call letters, WA2HEF, without looking them up: ·— ·· ·—·· ···· · ··—·.. However, Jeff was also changing as he began to embark on that dark, dangerous, yet exciting expedition of male pubescence, with all its inherent machinations. Nancy, bless her heart, was still running around the neighborhood with a towel stuck down the back of her slacks, pretending she was a horse.

We now know that my parents agonized over their decision to have Tom institutionalized. To have him sent to a state school meant that formal custody would be transferred to New York State. Mom and Dad would no longer be sole decision makers regarding Tom's care and well-being. At this time in history, both the mental health and the medical professions, by and large, strongly recommended institutional care for persons with Down syndrome. They believed institutional care gave the rest of the family more opportunities to meet their full potential while allowing trained professionals to care for the person with special needs. They made a convincing argument.

I have seen my mother cry maybe three times in my life. She grew up in a stoic Swiss-German household that didn't express much negative emotion. Mom loves to laugh, enjoys just about everyone, and is loved by one and all. Anything negative tends to get swept under the carpet as quickly as possible so that everyone can get back to having a nice time together. Tears are not shed willy-nilly; they are reserved for the big stuff. In the fall of 1961, she was confronted with the big stuff.

I remember the family conference where Dad presided. He was speaking pretty well, but choking up a little. Mom was sitting there with Tommy between them, silently sobbing as Dad relayed to us kids that Tom was going to move out of our house to live at this place called Rome State School.

A little slow to grasp what was actually being said, I remember asking, "You mean he's moving away from our home?" Yes. I heard it right. My bunkmate, playmate, partner-in-crime for the past nine years was leaving. For good. He was being abandoned.

"Will we ever be able to see him again?" I frantically asked.

We were all reassured that we could visit him and that Tom would come and visit us at Christmas for a week. Tears welled up in my eyes and I joined Mom in the sobbing department.

I remember the day Mom, Dad, and Tommy took off. They had Tom's clothes packed in a couple of suit cases, one of which was a hard shelled, orange American Tourister piece that Dad often used on his business trips. Tom shuffled out to the car, unsuspecting of what was going on. He was like a little lamb being led to slaughter. I don't remember exactly, but Mom must have asked Mrs. Panasik, an older woman who had emigrated from Czechoslovakia after the war, to watch over us after we got home from school. Mom and Dad returned from the six hour round-trip to Rome, New York, around supper time with an empty suitcase and empty hearts. There was a dullness to everything for weeks.

Sure, I had my own bedroom now, but it wasn't the same. Tom's little murmurings were nowhere to be heard except in the retreating recesses of my mind. Life would resume, but it would never quite be normal.

Thanksgiving was without Tom that year, and there wasn't much to be thankful for anyway. We ate turkey and watched Detroit get beat again by the Bears (some things never change). As Christmas approached though, a new anticipation grew as I thought about Tom coming home. It would be great. And so it was. Christmas was spectacular! We sang carols, put simple puzzles together, trimmed the Christmas tree, snitched Mom's cutout cookies, danced to show tunes together (Tom was the only dance instructor I've ever had, and I'm afraid it shows), sledded, and got crazy waiting to open presents under the Christmas tree. We had pillow fights (although they were pretty tame, as violence was never a strong suit of Tom's), watched TV together, played ball, and enjoyed all of the merriment.

Christmas came and went and then one day shortly thereafter, the suitcase came out. Up until that moment, I had never seen this expression on Tom's face before. It was a determined look augmented by some of the most strident, plaintive, pleading language I have ever heard.

"Mama—Gogo home!"

Interpretation: "Mom, I like it here. I don't want to leave. How 'bouts we just forget about this suitcase business, unpack the bag, and get back to normal. I mean, this Rome State place is really swell and there are some great folks there, but let's stay put. Okay?"

"Gogo home?"

Interpretation: "Come on, Mom. You're not really serious about me leaving are you? Are you?"

Then with complete eye contact, "Mama, Gogo home!"

Interpretation: "PLEASE, PLEASE, PLEASE DON'T SEND ME BACK THERE. PLEASE!"

I'm not sure there was ever a convict walking to the electric chair who could have sounded more convincing.

As he was led away to the car, he continued to jabber something I hope can never be translated. He continued to complain until put into his seat. He then turned silent. If he happened to meet Mom or Dad's eyes, he'd pop the question again. But mostly there was an aura of dejected resignation surrounding him.

"Gogo home."

"No Tom, you can't stay at home. We're taking you back to school."

Tom also brought something else home with him that first Christmas that we learned about shortly after his return from the holidays. Unbeknownst to us, Tom had contracted hepatitis A shortly before coming home. It was still in the incubation period when symptoms are not yet manifested, although still highly communicable. When Tom returned to Rome after Christmas, he began to develop symptoms. He was diagnosed and immediately quarantined in their infirmary. My family was notified about our exposure to the disease. Consequently we and neighbors who may have come in contact with him needed to get treated with some sort of new special hepatitis vaccine (gamma globulin). So, the whole family dutifully marched down to Dr. Angulo's office and bared their rumps.

I couldn't help thinking about Tommy. There he was, twelve years old, at this capital "I" institution that had over five thousand inmates, in an infirmary with no family, no mother, and no friends to visit or console him. I had no idea at the time what kind of symptoms he had to endure, but knew it wasn't fun. Frankly, I was scared. Hepatitis was one of the biggest words I knew and it sounded ominous. He probably had flu-like symptoms of nausea, headaches, body aches, and fever for up to a couple of weeks before his liver infection finally subsided.[13]

Several months later while visiting Tom at Rome, the folks were startled to see that he had lost some of his hair in patches. His former neatly trimmed crew-cut now began to look like a patchwork quilt. It looked terrible, but Tom didn't seem to mind at all. Give him a magazine and things were good. A year following, he got an atypical relapse of hepatitis and was sequestered at the Rome State Infirmary yet again. This kid was taking a pounding! He recovered from that too, but his liver must have been screaming! The hair loss was a bit of a mystery in that it is not a typical symptom of the disease. By all rights, it is amazing that he survived, let alone lived until he was almost sixty. When he was born in 1949, the average life expectancy of a person with Down syndrome was twenty.[14]

Upon further investigation, I have learned that in the late 1950s and early 1960s, there was some funny business going on in at least a couple of the New York State schools for the retarded that were of questionable ethics. At a sister institution in Staten Island named Willowbrook, similar hepatitis outbreaks had regularly occurred throughout the period. It is common for hepatitis A to work its way around large inmate populations. It is easily spread through poor hygiene after using the toilet and the passage of infected fecal matter by contact (it is also transmitted from anal intercourse—if you need to know). What is not common, though, is for healthy persons, especially with developmental disabilities, to be intentionally infected with the virus so that the efficacy of new vaccines could be tested. It came to light in the mid-1960s that residents at Willowbrook were being used as human guinea pigs for invasive scientific experiments.[15] These people were unknowing test pilots in planes with only one wing. Could these experiments also have been happening at Rome State at the same time?

Equally disturbing was the disclosure by some investigative reporting of state institutions for the retarded that experiments with radioactive isotopes were being infused into children's milk for another scientific study on the effects of ionizing radiation. The parents/guardians were only told that their children would be in a test where they would be given extra milk. They were not told that this milk would be laced with toxic chemicals.[16] Better living through science. I hope that these experiments had nothing to do with Tom's unexplained permanent hair loss.

Every time I look at some of the research I've done on Rome State School, I get depressed. It was not a happy place for many of the residents (Tom included, I'm afraid). In addition to the developmentally disabled persons, there were also emotionally disturbed children with behavioral issues, not to mention people with serious mental illnesses. From what I can gather, it sounds like Rome State School also served as an orphanage for children who either had no family or were unwanted by their families of origin. Rules were strictly enforced and there were documented cases of neglect and abuse. In 1965, Senator Robert Kennedy toured several New York State institutions, including Rome State School. His report stated that the residents were living in dehumanizing conditions. Regarding Willowbrook, he called it a "snake pit."[17]

Staff at both Rome and Willowbrook took umbrage at the accusations, but a separate investigation from then Governor Rockefeller confirmed what Kennedy had reported. Coincidental with Kennedy's report, there was also an investigatory photo essay published by Dr. Burton Blatt and Fred Kaplan entitled *Christmas in Purgatory*.[18] Pictures were taken with a concealed camera that identified deplorable conditions. The essay was specifically about the Willowbrook facility, but also implicated Rome State School. Even Geraldo Rivera got into the act and put a much touted TV documentary/exposé together for ABC television. Michael Wilkens, a staff doctor at Willowbrook, piqued Rivera's interest when he stated, "In my building, there are sixty retarded kids, with only one attendant to take care of them. Most are naked and they lie in their own shit."[19]

With a peak inmate population in the early '60s, New York State, along with the rest of the country, began the slow process of reforming its mental health institutions. States started treating persons with mental or physical disabilities a little differently. For starters, they began segregating dangerous persons from non-dangerous residents. States also began trying to find smaller institutions or group homes for those who could manage without heavy-handed supervision. Our country began to wake up and offer at least some of the privileges of American citizenship to all of its family, friends, and neighbors. In 1989, Rome State School was closed as an institution for the mentally retarded and, shortly thereafter, reopened as a medium security prison. Enough said!

The back-story of how Western civilization has treated the physically and mentally disadvantaged is an interesting, if not terrifying epic, but it is not my intention to address that in this book. Suffice to say, society's attitudes and management of people with mental disabilities significantly affected my family. When we visited Tom at Rome State School, we typically saw caring staff taking care of their charges. We didn't know about any of the scary stuff at the time, thank goodness. Knowing about these aspects of neglect now makes me cringe, not just for our family, but also for thousands of others. I'd like to think that it was just a small fraction of children and patients who were subject to abuse. However, we now know that there was significant care that could be termed marginal at best.

Along with his visits home, our family made periodic visits to see Tom at Rome. Rome State School was an impressive campus. It was comparable to a medium sized college campus with buildings ranging from new to what architectural historians might call "turn of the century scary institutional." I remember the main administration building as one of the older ones and located at the end of a leafy entry lane from the nearby highway. Like many Victorian buildings of that era, the main floor was approached by a formidable exterior flight of stairs up to a grand porch that led to hefty oak entry doors. These doors were oppressively large and intimidating. Architecturally they dictated, "Bow before you enter!"

Every visitor checked-in at the main administration building. Behind the reception desk where we requested permission to have Tom sent out to us was a recreation hall. On one occasion, while I was waiting for an orderly to bring Tom down, I recall watching two fellows in their teens playing ping pong—or at least their version of it. It was a hotly contested scrimmage, with much banter and lead changes that were mind boggling. When I started eavesdropping on the game, I believe the score was five to eight. The server hit the ball but it completely missed the table—six points for the server. After chasing down the ball the opponent went to serve and missed the ball entirely. That was good for twenty points for somebody. I watched for about five minutes with the score bouncing as much as the ball. There was another lead change, then another, and amazing point swings with almost no contact with either the ball or the ball with the table. Excitement was palpable though and I knew that the winner would be decided with the last play. With the score tightly knotted-up at thirty-five to thirty-five, the final serve was made (I was the only one who didn't know it was the final serve). The server made contact and the ball went bouncing into the corner. Game over! Twenty-five to 'F'. Both contestants congratulated each other on a good game and a hard fought battle and started up a new match. It was at this point that I made the initial connection that winning at everything maybe wasn't the goal for a happy life. If you could have as much fun as these guys and not really care who came away with the trophy, maybe success had a broader definition.

With an attitude like that towards sports, no wonder these individuals needed to be kept away from mainstream American culture.

In the winter, we traveled up for day visits and usually brought our sleds along. Somewhere in one of the residential areas of Rome there was a great sledding hill. It was perfect. It was a long relatively steep slope that always had lots of snow because Rome is part of the snow belt of central New York. With Lake Ontario to the North and Lake Erie to the West, Rome was nicely positioned to have ample moisture conspire with Canadian cold fronts that regularly ignored the border.

We had a couple of Flexible Flyer sleds that were marginally steerable and an aluminum Flying Saucer, which was just a concave piece of aluminum that had no steer-ability whatsoever. The saucer should have come with a permanently attached statue of St. Christopher and a kneeling pad as every trip down was a suicide mission. The rider did not know what or whom they might run into as, by design, the disc would immediately rotate such that you were always going down the hill backwards. There were Kamikaze pilots who refused to set their butts in these things, preferring instead a plane highly loaded with explosive ordnance and only a half tank of fuel.

Tom was a fearless saucer rider, though. His low center of gravity and his ability to sit in a stable lotus position (knees crossed with both feet finding an opposite thigh to rest on) gave him an advantage over many others, like me. In contrast, I was light, top heavy, and bouncy. I would take the saucer down and be somewhere in the middle of the hill saying a prayer for deliverance, traveling backwards, hurtling blindly through space (like an old Mercury space capsule on re-entry) when I'd hit a snow jump. These were made by some kid, the type who would ride their sleds standing up, hit the jump, and land without falling (you know the type) at the steepest part of the hill. I'd hit the same bump unprepared, of course, because I couldn't see it. I'd then explode into a fireworks display of arms and legs going in all directions before crashing, tumbling, and burning to a crisp.

When it came time to pull the sleds up the hill, guess whose job it was? What a crock. I was getting manipulated and I felt abused. After a successful ride down the hill, Tom stood up by his sled or saucer and waited for the next available lift back up the slope.

"Taxi! Oh Taxi!"

I'd take one of his hands in mine and then with two sleds in the other hand, shuttle everything back up to the crest of the hill. I suppose I should be thankful he didn't make me pull him up with him seated on his sled.

Tom didn't do sleds uphill, thank you very much.

Summertime visits to Rome usually entailed a trip to Verona Beach on Oneida Lake, one of the Finger Lakes scattered along the central region of New York. It is also a part of the Erie Canal route from Lake Erie to Albany to New York City. Geography and history lesson aside, when we got to the lakeside park, we changed into our swim suits at a beach house, ate a picnic lunch Mom had prepared (sandwiches, potato chips, candy bars, and soda pop), and headed off to the water. We usually brought an air mattress and a couple of inner tubes to float around on and ride the waves. Tom was good at getting into a used, patched inner tube and hanging onto it, bobbing to his heart's content for the afternoon.

On one memorable summer day at Verona Beach, a brief storm came from almost nowhere. A strong squall line picked up thirty mile an hour winds and sent all of the beach goers skittering for protection. We closed the picnic basket, grabbed the beach towels, and ran (Tom plodded) for the car. We were several yards from the car when the wall of wind hit us. To our consternation, every mayfly larva had hatched that day on Oneida Lake and they formed a dense, black cloud with the initial blast. We were pelted by the thousands in our final dash to the car, getting them in our mouth, ears, swim trunks, towels, and then when the car doors opened, into every nook and cranny of the automobile. Inside the car's cabin, some were still flying around while the dead were piling up. It was like the coolest thing I'd ever experienced in my life up to that point. The only downside was that the car stunk for several weeks as we would find yet another pile of decaying mayflies we had missed removing earlier.

Whether it was a winter, spring, summer, or fall visit, Tom knew when the day was about over and he'd start the questioning,

"Mama. Gogo home?!"

With the exception of that episode with a full load of dead and dying mayflies, the return trip from Rome was empty and quiet.

Tom was a resident of Rome State School from 1961 until 1971. In January of 1971, my folks moved across the country from New York to the Pacific Northwest. Tom's guardianship was subsequently transferred to the State of Washington and they placed him in a facility not far from Spokane called Lakeland Village at Medical Lake. It was smaller in scale than Rome and with far fewer residents. Although it had a similar history of housing the criminally insane and feeble minded, reforms had advanced to the point that the facility primarily cared for developmentally disabled persons by the time Tom arrived. On college breaks and visits to Medical Lake, I found the staff to be at ease and very caring. Tom was able to visit my parents' home frequently and when his weekend furlough was over, his desperate protests were rarely heard. He'd simply gather up a few magazines and find his spot in the back seat of the car, signaling that he was ready and willing to make the trip back to Lakeland Village.

In the 1980s, the folks moved back to the Midwest. Dad was now an independent educational consultant, which allowed the folks the opportunity to live anywhere. As they had both grown up in Iowa and as my brother was then teaching at Iowa State University, they chose to relocate to Ames. Tom was accepted into a small residential group home for persons with developmental disabilities. Nirvana! Tom shared a nice ranch-style house with four or five housemates and a number of caring attendants. At his home, he had his own bedroom and pretty much the run of the house (within limits). Staff taught him to communicate better, fix simple meals, help with household chores, and become an active part of the community. He even attended classes where he learned many new physical and cognitive skills.

Tom also became employed (about time)! He, along with many of his buddies, held several jobs including stuffing utility bills for the City of Ames and putting rubber "O" rings on something or other for a local manufacturer. Tom was methodical about his work. That is to say he did a great job at what he did, but just didn't do a whole lot of it without a little encouragement. The repetitive nature of the work fit him well.

I recall visiting Tom at the sheltered workshop one day and watched the assembly line in progress with "Mr. Entrepreneur" doing his thing. He'd stuff an envelope, rock back in his chair, admire his handiwork, fold the sealing flap over two or three times, then set it face up and neatly stacked for the sealer to complete the process. One done!

"Tom, let's keep going," one of the attendants would kindly prompt.

He'd look over at his manager, Jerilyn, smile a big grin with his characteristic crinkly eyes, wave, then pick up another bill and another envelope. In slow motion he'd insert the next bill, making sure the customer's address showed through the envelope's window. He might then pull the statement back outside of the envelope and rein-sert it a time or two just to make sure it was properly posi-tioned for the next step. A couple of flips of the envelope flap, back and forth, and voila, another masterpiece. Two done! Time to sit back, admire and take a coffee break.

Tom was also an expert O-ring put-er on-er. I never found out exactly what he was putting rubber "O" rings on, but I remember when the Space Shuttle Challenger tragically blew up on lift-off, the cause had been a fuel leak past an "O" ring between sections on the booster rocket. I remember thinking that this couldn't possibly have been Tom's "O" ring because he would have been rolling it into—then out of—position about a hundred times before finally determining that it had been installed correctly. I have no doubt that whatever tool, instrument, or sub-assembly Tom was working on, that his particular "O" ring had never been so totally and completely scrutinized.

Tom was paid for his work too. Payment was by the piece, so some of his paychecks cost way more to process than the amount for which they were written. I had never before seen a paycheck cut for $0.37. I always wished that I could have witnessed the bank teller's face when Tom went to endorse it.

"I'm sorry, Mr. Prater, but that scribble doesn't seem to match the one we have on file."

Tom's needs were taken care of at his house so his earn-ings were luxuriously squandered once a month on a new magazine or two.

Tom's group home for the last twenty-five years of his life was truly his home. There was no apprehension, ever, about returning after a visit with the folks. As a matter of fact, on the Sunday of a weekend visit, he'd start ask-ing about his housemates as if to say, "I need to get back now. Danny probably needs me." His buddies there were every bit his family. His family became our family too, as we'd visit and occasionally have birthday celebrations at his house. Cake, ice cream, and the world's most discordant, raucous, out-of-tune rendition of "Happy Birthday" were enthusiastically shared. Few celebrations could rival such heartfelt simplicity.

Tom bounced around a lot as he lived his life from home to one institution after another. He moved from the east coast to the west and eventually landed in the middle. Tom's health went from great to periods of serious illness and isolation. Through it all though, he finally ended up exactly where he needed to be.

As the Shaker dancing song *Simple Gifts* relates,

'Tis a gift to be simple, tis a gift to be free
'Tis the gift to come down where we ought to be,
And when we find ourselves in the place just right,
'Twill be in the valley of love and delight.

When true simplicity is gain'd,
To bow and to bend we shan't be asham'd,
To turn, turn, will be our delight,
Till by turning, turning we come 'round right.

CHAPTER 7

Trips with Tom

"One thousand bottles of beer on the wall
One thousand bottles of beer,
Take one down, pass it around,
Nine hundred ninety-nine bottles of beer on the wall.
Nine hundred ninety-nine bottles of beer on the wall..."
(keep singing until you get to Iowa)

Author unknown

To Iowa

"I want to hear two grunts and a splash!" the voice echoed around the linoleum tiled upstairs hall.

It was Dad, turned drill sergeant, making an unjust demand of sleepy sphincters at 4:00 am. Dutifully we'd climb up on the toilet and start trying to pinch something out—anything. Still red in the face, we'd pass the baton to the next sibling waiting their turn for their moment on the throne. Usually nothing came, but it was the effort that really mattered. Dad did not want to have to stop the car fifteen minutes from home with some sniveling kid complaining that they needed to go to the bathroom and then having to stop at a greasy filling station with grimy gray fixtures, no toilet paper, floating remnants from previous pilgrims in the toilet bowel, and a soap dispenser (they looked like tiny hot air balloons) devoid of green semi-radioactive soap. The Oldsmobile had been packed the night before and this was the final boarding call for all ticketed passengers.

"Arrrggghhh!!" Plip.

Before Nancy came along, Jeff and I had the rear bench seat, unencumbered with seat belts, to ourselves. Tommy was perched on an unrestrained small wooden box in the front between Mom and Dad. Often in the pre-sister era, our trips would start Friday night. We'd leave as soon as Dad got home from work when IBM closed down for two weeks in July. Mom had already packed the car, a 1950 Dodge sedan, and made sandwiches, snacks, and a tall thermos of coffee, ready to hit the road. Dad changed out of his suit and off we went to Iowa, home to grandparents and a bunch of aunts, uncles, and cousins. It was a thirty-hour marathon over mostly two lane highways through every major Rust Belt City between Binghamton, New York, and Dubuque, Iowa. The route included Rochester, Buffalo, Erie, Cleveland, Toledo, South Bend, and the yellow orange skies of Gary, Indiana. We made an overnight stay with one of Mom's brothers in a western suburb of Chicago and then we'd be off to Dubuque and Webster City, Iowa.

I'm told that there was a mattress jerry-rigged in the backseat for Jeff and me to hypothetically sleep on. I don't remember sleeping, but I do remember muffled voices heard over road noises and seeing lights always flashing around from passing vehicles. I recollect Tom stoically sitting between Mom and Dad dangling a cloth for twenty-four hours straight. I'm guessing he must have leaned against Mom's shoulder for a quick wink or two, or maybe even been shuffled to the back with Jeff and me, but I don't remember that. I remember seeing the silhouette of his head with his bent ears and a glimpse of a dangling cloth.

He was vigilant and I don't blame him. I mean, there he sat with the folks, a mere three feet from the windscreen, with no restraint system save my Dad's right arm. Dad would instinctively hold that protective limb out like a train crossing guard-arm upon any kind of rapid decelera-tion. In a serious accident, I can envision his arm still held out in front of Tom while the three of them simultaneously flew out the front windshield together. In a rollover the backseat occupants would have joined them in a wicked jumble, like those painted ping pong balls in the tumbling cage they use for picking lottery numbers.

"All very safe," we were assured by the motor car com-panies of the day. After all, how could anyone get hurt in a vehicle surrounded by enough steel to rival the weight of a Sherman Tank? Believe it or not, people still got hurt, and pretty regularly. In 1950, one was seven times more likely to be killed or injured in an automobile as measured against similar statistics gathered in 2013. The records show that there were 7.24 fatalities per every million vehicle miles traveled compared with 1.11 fatalities in 2013.[20] Seat belts (which Dad installed before they were mandated), divided highways, tires that somehow rarely fail, front and side airbags, along with other safety innovations have made speeding around at seventy miles per hour significantly safer. Safety has since taken a huge step backwards with the advent of the cellular telephone, but I won't confuse anyone with any more statistics.

However, up until the mid-1960s, with no seatbelts in cars, kids were allowed to roam the cabin like free range chickens. We climbed over the front seat-back, laid down on the generous ledge under the rear window, played on the floor of the leg wells, stood-up on the edge of the rear seat while leaning on the back of the front seat, cranked windows down, cranked them up, and used the seat as a trampoline. While speeding along, one could also easily unlock a door (presuming it was locked in the first place) and open it to spit or pour out the remains of a soda. (Note: The Lincoln Continental Town Car's rear doors, nicknamed "suicide doors," conveniently hinged on the back side of the rear door so that if a back seat occupant opened it while moving, it acted as an air scoop. If one were traveling fast enough, it ripped the door from its hinges and took along whatever arm had opened it for a ride down the turnpike.)

Occasionally, our driver distraction program would be rudely interrupted with, "Don't make me stop this car!" or a blind swipe from the driver's free hand. But normal play (i.e. no fighting or screaming) was allowed. Some taunting or teasing could also be tolerated up to the point where my sister would say in a bratty, tattle-tale voice, "Mommmmm, Steve's on my side of the seat." Nancy eventually grew out of her nagging kid-sister phase, or maybe I grew out of my tormenting big-brother stage. In any event, we can now travel upwards of fifty miles together without poking at one another. Please don't hold me to that though.

On those marathon trips to Iowa, Mom was good at keeping us occupied during the daylight hours. We'd sing camp songs, do finger plays, and when we were old enough, play the alphabet game. This is where you tried to go through the alphabet, character by character, looking for road signs that began with the appointed letter. It was always fun until we got to "Q" and couldn't find a Quaker State Oil sign. We'd get bored with looking and resume our driver distraction tactics.

McDonald's was still mostly a twinkle in Ray Kroc's eyes, so eating a meal meant either a roadside diner or, more than likely, a sandwich from a picnic basket Mom had packed to be eaten at some fly infested picnic table along US 20 some-where in Indiana (I don't mean to pick on Indiana—Iowa and Illinois had similar flies). The picnic tabletop was usually splattered white from local birds that had also seen fit to use this particular table for their purposes. Mom, ever prepared, had a vinyl tablecloth to spread out before the picnic began. I appreciated the fact that we were covering bird poop with this tablecloth, but it still bothered me that just because we put food on one side and the bird poop was on the other, weren't we still cross-contaminating things when we folded up the tablecloth after the picnic and put it back into the basket? I can't think about it too long. I hope Mom has since burned that thing, but I doubt it.

To this day, Mom still packs picnic lunches to take along with us on short road trips. She does this without thinking. Here she is, the ninety-two year old mama bear still taking care of papa bear and sixty-plus-year-old cubs. If we need to travel more than two hours anywhere, she breaks out a 1960s plaid vinyl zippered tote bag that has a coffee thermos and a long plastic box, into which she packs three peanut butter and jellies and a couple of bologna sandwiches. There will be potato chips, fun-size candy bars, a dozen chocolate chip cookies, and a standing rib roast. It is like a magic act where she keeps pulling stuff out of a top hat until we're full or get to our destination. What a way to travel.

I have known some families that do not allow any eating in their cars at all. What a shame! Our family traveled on food as much as the car traveled on gasoline. If Mom wasn't dealing snacks, there were always Cheerios or maybe M&M's to be dug out from behind the seat cushion.

While bouncing around at sixty miles an hour, Tom was always first to respond when Mom would ask if someone would like something to eat. It was uncanny how fast he replied, almost as if he had been waiting, lurking, preparing all along for Mom to ask,

"Would anyone like..."

"Yeah! Yeah! Me! Me! Tom Prater, Tom Prater!"
"...a cookie?"

Tom was like a gun slinger at high noon when it came to responding to a food offer. Hands at his side, hovering over his six-shooters, fingers twitching, steely glint in his eye, tumbleweed bouncing past, patrons peeking out from behind swinging saloon doors...

"Go ahead, punk, just try to get your entire question out!"
"How about a sna...
                    KA-POW
                                ...ack?"

To the Lake

Late in the summer, when the grass began to turn brown and the kiddie pool just wouldn't do, we'd begin a conspiracy to get the folks to take us swimming at Quaker Lake. It didn't take much persuasion, as the folks were just as miserable as we were with no air conditioning or a place to get cooled down other than this spring-fed lake about twenty-five minutes south of town.

We'd invite a couple of friends while preparations were made. Mom, of course, made sandwiches and lemonade and Dad pumped up old patched inner tubes for floatation devices (meeting all safety regulations, I'm sure). We kids changed into swim suits. The kids were ready long before Dad's tired arms had finished pumping up three or four inner tubes so we'd wait and try to get hotter. The theory was that if we were really, *really* hot, it wouldn't take us as long to get used to the frigid water of Quaker Lake. Sometimes we'd sit in the closed car for a few minutes and bake. Our own solar sauna, so to speak. Nobody's IQ was over the top in our group and none realized that we could have given ourselves heat stroke.

Eventually everyone piled into the car. Mom, Tom, and Dad in the front as usual, then Jeff, Nancy, me, Bob, Ellen, Chris, Karen, Carol, Chuck, and maybe a few others in the back. Then a couple of inner tubes, goggles, fins, beach balls, and air mattresses (that couldn't fit in the trunk) were jammed into the backseat. Although by today's standards this would be considered unsafe (and perhaps illegal), we were participating in a test for prototype airbags. Had there been an accident, pre-inflated inner-tubes would have absorbed most of the shock, at least for back seat occupants.

Upon arrival at the lake, the car doors swung open and we'd explode out of the automobile like compressed springs finally set free, running wildly to the beach. The beach had railroad ties piled on top of each other, two-high, to form a little wall. Our sweating, over-heated bodies yearning to cool down would all of a sudden stop at the wall between the grass and the water, as a trial toe would broadcast back to the brain, "Way too cold—WARNING—Way too cold!" So we would sit on a railroad tie and ease in. As one foot would numb-up the other would follow until we were in the ice bath and wading out deeper. We waded into water just below our swimming trunks and the ever "sensitive skin" area it covered. There we stood, water just below our crotches, and waited for courage to make the final plunge and complete the cool down. We'd hop around on tiptoes like nincompoops while a few splashes of water dampened our trunks. We tried to dodge splashes from those who had already committed, yelling at them to stop and pledging revenge until the death of them. Finally, when trunks were thoroughly soaked, the moment was right and we'd bob down to our chins. A final sizzling sound confirmed that the steam our bodies had generated all day was finally extinguished. Aaaahhhh!

Mom and Dad pretended not to make a big deal about the water temperature. They waded in up to about their knees and then made a forward dive, creating a splash that seemed enormous. They saved their dignity this way. I later learned that even with adult fur, they also had the same sensitivity issues, but just got it over with faster and more maturely. I'm sure they were screaming underwater but you can't usually hear those screams unless you listen carefully.

Tom entered into the water with no hesitation whatsoever. Completely ensconced in a tube of black rubber, he stood on the creosoted pier and without pausing, jumped in. Tom gave no indication of any discomfort. He latched onto the side of the inner tube and paddled about until his toes turned to raisins, shriveled and wrinkled from overexposure to what he termed "Sffffwwimminn." He never learned to really swim or float and panicked if his face somehow went underwater. But as long as he was in his tube, he was the dreadnaught on the lake and the happiest aquanaut ever.

The Whee Hill

By whee, I do not mean wee. I mean, "Wheeeeeeeeee!"

In the mid-1950s through the mid-1960s, Dad traveled quite a bit on business for IBM. He was an electrical engineer and had been hired by Big Blue right after World War II. He was caught in the computing frenzy that mushroomed then and continues to this day. IBM's world headquarters was in Endicott, New York, but they were frantically building and increasing in size weekly. Their stature as a small business machine outfit making time clocks, teletype machines, typewriters, and punch clocks jumped exponentially when they got into mainframe computing and developing all of the software applications that would go with these impressive blinking electronic wizards. For a couple of decades they had a stranglehold on mainframe computing, until 1969 when an antitrust suit was filed against them by the Justice Department. Although the case was eventually dismissed, it seemed to allow more competition. Then when personal computers started gaining widespread use, Big Blue began to share pieces of the computing revenue pie a little more equitably. Today, IBM has mostly reverted to main-frame applications and they have left the personal computing market to the piranhas.

In the meantime, Dad was flying several times a year to venues on both coasts as well as downstate New York. As Endicott and the Triple Cities are close to nowhere, his flights would originate from a small county airport built on the top of a hill in northern Broome County. American Airlines and Eastern Airlines flew regularly scheduled flights in and out of Broome County, but it was Mohawk Airlines, a regional carrier out of Utica, New York, that handled the largest volume. Mohawk transported a lot of passengers to New York City's airports for transference to longer national and international flights. In the 1950s, Mohawk's fleet was mostly Douglas DC 3's. We often watched Dad grab one of those thirty-two seats on the tail-dragger (no nose gear) and head off the mountain-top, usually pointed for a New York City area airport like LaGuardia, Idlewild, or Newark.

We kids would stand, fingers clutched through chain link fence, on the outside observation platform above the boarding gate. We'd then shout and wave at Dad as he walked across the tarmac and watch as he stooped slightly to enter the little arch-topped metal door near the tail of the plane. With the door securely shut, a ground crew member rolled out a huge fire extinguisher and parked it next to the engine to be started. Then (and airports don't provide this kind of entertainment anymore) the guy with this man-sized fire extinguisher twirled a finger in the air, giving the pilot the signal to fire-up that engine. The three bladed prop whined a little as it made its first rotation or two. Then, wheezing and coughing, the engine engaged and blue smoke and fire belched out of the exhaust manifold before the newly developed prop wash could push it all away. They repeated the same process on the starboard engine and with both engines running smoothly, the pilot taxied to the runway for take-off. Take-off was always exciting too. At night you could actually see little blue flames exiting the manifolds from the engines as it lifted off and climbed into the darkened sky. Wow!

Having never flown, we wondered what it must feel like to break the bonds of the earth. We often queried Dad upon his arrival as to how cool it was up in the sky.

"Was it bumpy?"

"Did you lose your stomach?"

"How far could you see?"

"What's it like to be in a cloud?"

"Did it hurt when the plane landed?"

"Could you see the Empire State Building?"

"What gift did you bring me?"

If Dad had a particularly early or late flight, he usually took the limousine shuttle to the airport or brought it home. Most often, though, Mom loaded us into the Oldsmobile "Rocket 88" to retrieve him at the terminal. Picking up Dad was important to us kids for four reasons. First, we missed him and looked forward to seeing him after having run rough-shod over Mother for upwards of a week. Second, there might just be an outside chance of being the recipient of a gift or trinket as we, his poor children, had suffered so without the firm but loving direction of our wonderful Father. Third, my brother Jeff and I were nuts about anything to do with airplanes (I am still unjustly accused of this from some family members). And finally, there was the "whee" hill.

The Whee hill was our equivalent to a roller coaster. It was a small rise in the Farm-to-Market Road followed by a somewhat rapid dip. Traveling at twenty or twenty-five miles per hour, this was hardly recognizable as anything other than another up and down in the road. However, when traveling a little faster and goosing the accelerator right at the crest of the hill, one would get the feeling of being launched from a battleship's naval gun. We'd all laugh with delight, but it became evident early on that Tom particularly enjoyed his one-second weightless ride in space.

Upon hearing that we were going to pick up Dad at the airport, Tom would begin to anticipate.

"Ahhport. Oh boy!"

He'd get in a trance-like stupor, looking at nothing in particular, then his lips would go into jabber mode (moving but no audible sound), his head would wag a few times (you could see it building), he'd scrunch up (contracting his arms into his body and his hands into fists), his eyes would disappear into his cheeks, and then he'd shake all over while detonating with a giddy squeal of laughter. This was a whole body event and we hadn't even gotten into the car yet. I have to confess I took great pleasure in prodding this behavior out of him and getting Tom all keyed-up. It probably wasn't ethically correct for me to do that to him, but the infectious glee it left me with wouldn't let me stop. Also, I was his brother and I had a license to do it.

As we approached the take-off point in the car, we went through our check-off list.

"Speed increasing from twenty-five?"

Check.

"Tires properly inflated?"

Probably.

"Seatbelts?"

What seatbelts?

Five seconds before liftoff, Jeff, Nancy, and I would start into the pre-whee wind-up. Starting as low as our soprano voices would allow, we'd begin the wwwwwwhhhhhhhhhhhHHHHHHHHHHHHHHH hitting the EEEEEEEEEEE syllable molto fortissimo at the critical point of departure. Tom would be beside himself and we'd all be laughing hysterically except Mom, who dutifully kept her eyes on the road but whose slight smile betrayed her complicit participation in our conspiracy with her right foot's little touch of gas at just the right moment.

Tom was a great traveler. He never whined or complained. He didn't fight. He could sit quietly for hours without muttering a word while looking at the same magazine. Feed him a snack from time to time and you wouldn't even know he was there.

In 1971, Jeff and I drove back to the Midwest from New York after our college Christmas breaks. We had his VW Beetle packed full when we were reminded that we needed to drop Tom off at Rome on our way. So we went about carving-out about a sixteen inch square spot in the already claustrophobic back seat. When it was time to leave, Tom joyfully squeezed into his spot as if he were getting into a tiny barrel ready to make the plunge over Niagara Falls. We stopped once on the four and one-half hour trip to Rome, but other than that he just sat there quietly dangling a cloth. When asked how he was doing, he'd lean forward, reach out a finger, and say, "I'm warm." Everything was perfect in his five cubic feet of space. If airlines could find such compliant, comfortable, agreeable passengers, they would probably be able to squeeze another sixty passengers on each flight. God forbid!

CHAPTER 8

Keeping up Appearances

"He isn't very handsome
And he isn't very tall
But he has a heart as big can be
And a love for one and all."

—Peter Pan Records ("Popeye")

When Tom was young, he was the poster child for the phrase, "Cuter than a bug's ear." Until about eleven or twelve years of age, he was a good looking young chap. He had brown hair, always sporting a crisp crew cut (courtesy of Dad's basement barbershop) on a smallish, trim, physique. Typical of many Down syndrome children, he was not very muscular, but then again, neither were his brothers. His adult height may have been 5'-0" so when he stood between Jeff and me when we were in college and high school, respectively, either his torso or our heads were regularly truncated in family pictures. He had a nice smile if you didn't ask him to smile (if you did ask, you needed to be prepared for a scrunched up face). He exhibited many of the common physical traits associated with Downs syndrome, including the characteristic slanted eyes (one of which was also crossed). He had a broad flat face, a short nose that bent to the right from a deviated septum, and the typical thick rough tongue that thrust out regularly. He also had delicate hands with relatively short fingers. Tom could run a little, but usually there was never much hurry in him so he tended to plod with his head down when he walked. It was discernable that he was a little different—but not that different.

In the 1950s and '60s, one got dressed up to go to church on Sunday. Sport coats and ties were the standard for men and boys, with skirts or dresses for the ladies. So it was in our household. Dad taught me how to tie a neck tie when I was about nine and although Tom couldn't tie his own, you could tell by his demeanor that he liked getting spiffed-up. We Prater boys looked pretty darn good on Sunday morning, if I do say so myself (Nancy always looked good). In our hearts we could be playing football, messing around in the mud, teasing girls, making mischief of all sorts, but on the outside we looked sharp. There is a vivid picture in my mind of a photograph Dad took of Tom shortly before he left home for Rome State School. He was standing next to a section of what remained of the backyard fence. One of his arms was propped on it with the other in his sport coat pocket, his crisp cuffed trousers housing legs that were casually crossed at the ankle (reminiscent of one of those classic photos of the Kennedys at Hyannis port). On his shoulders he wore a grey tweed sport coat with a Scottish plaid wool tie against a perfectly pressed white shirt. This guy exuded the essence of the term debonair. If he had more hair than a crew cut allowed, he could have been in a Brylcreem ad. Put a pipe in his hand and let him loose in Esquire magazine!

Then things started falling apart. It started when he went away to school and left Mother's guidance. Prior to his departure, Mom always made sure that he was adequately presentable. This concept didn't just apply to Tom but to Jeff and me as well. If I had not had Mom's exhortations and admonitions to comb my hair or change my socks, who knows what I would look like today. For starters I'd probably still be wearing the same flannel shirt I wore in 1970 (not that I see anything wrong with that).

Anyway, some of Tom's suave Gentleman's Quarterly qualities began to slip. Rome State School was not the Bon Marché nor a fashion design institute. I got the feeling that fashion and coiffure was not a curriculum offered by the state. Personal grooming and hygiene began to enter a tail-spin.

Some of Tom's appearance was not his fault. Getting hepatitis is not something anyone sets out to do. We think it caused him to lose his hair in a willy-nilly fashion, with an undiscerning tuft here and there. It was like his scalp was being attacked with explosives. When I first saw him, I was aghast. It was all patchy. This was not male pattern baldness and it wasn't the thinning of hair that often accompanies radiation treatment. It was like looking down on a forest where some sections of trees had been clear-cut while others not. There was no haircut that could fix it. Add to that the jaundiced skin that accompanies hepatitis A and you have a sorry looking camper (the jaundice was only temporary).

Tom eventually regrew his hair only to lose it again from a relapse a year after his first bout with hepatitis. Hair follicles, not willing to give up without a fight, would try to re-establish lost ground. Over the years, though, they finally just gave up trying. By the time he was thirty, the battle was over and Tom was as bald as a:

A) Billiard Ball;
B) Bowling ball;
C) "Mr. T";
D) All of the above
(Answer at the end of the chapter)

At one point in the mid-1970s, my folks tried having him wear a hairpiece. The intentions were good in that they didn't want one more physical condition to be a reason for others to stare at him. This attempt was not successful. Maybe if he had been wearing a leisure suit with a wide lapelled shirt open to his waist the effect would have been different. But as it was, Tom didn't care for the fuzzy look and the toupee would often sit lop-sided on his head. The toupee idea was abandoned and Tom picked-up, along with Yul Brenner and Telly Savalas, the "I'm Bald and Proud of It" movement, copied so indiscriminately these days by mere novices in professional sports who have to shave their heads and think that blue (or green or red or purple) skin is attractive. Amateurs!

Teeth were another thing that Tom had trouble hanging onto. He began to lose them in Rome, continued in the State of Washington, and they were nearly gone by the time he moved to Ames, Iowa. I don't know if he lost teeth as a result of poor dental hygiene, bad genetics, a side effect from hepatitis or the consumption of five tons of marshmallows in an earlier life. However, when added to the loss of his hair, Tom's condition was disheartening to say the least. You could always cover a bare skull by putting on a stocking cap or a coat of Turtle Wax, but losing teeth meant that something wasn't going to get chewed before entering the digestive tract, not to mention that you started looking like something out of a Charles Dickens novel or the movie *Deliverance*.

The first teeth to go were the lower incisors, then the uppers, the lateral incisors, the canines, bicuspids, and eventually the molars. It seemed to me that every time I would see him in high school or college, he would be waiting for his next payment from the tooth fairy. I think he was working with two remaining molars for about the last ten years of his life. Tom, however, was absolutely unconcerned about the whole thing. He was certain he would have enough teeth to do what needed to be done. If there weren't enough teeth, there were always gums.

While he was living in Washington State, some dentures were made for him. This seemed like an excellent idea at the time, but alas, he couldn't keep them in place to save his soul. I don't know how much adhesive was used, but I don't think there was enough Fixodent on the west coast to keep those things aligned. He'd talk or try to eat and they would clap and click like castanets in a mariachi band percussion section. He'd try to smile with them and he'd look like Teddy Roosevelt—way too many teeth visible for a normal smile. With that many bright, white teeth, his hair piece, and a good leisure suit, he could have been a part of the group closing on the Lawrence Welk Show. I can see him now, standing on the stage next to Norma Zimmer looking up at her with adoring eyes and then clicking through his teeth, "Noohma."

The teeth and hair piece ended up being discarded or taken to Goodwill or whatever one does with "falsies" when you are done with them. Tom was happier and somehow food still got masticated sufficiently to digest and provide nourishment for the next thirty years, with the added benefit that there was no amount of sugar he could ingest that would compromise teeth he didn't have. How he avoided diabetes, I'll never know. When Tom was at home for dinner, we followed a careful regimen of cutting food into small pieces, especially meat. Without many teeth to grind with, choking was always a concern. If you sat next to Tom, you knew it was your job to make sure the food was sufficiently diced and to keep an eye on his eating progress.

A common characteristic of Down syndrome is a propensity for obesity. This is probably a result of weaker muscle tone, shorter, stubbier limbs and a less robust heart muscle. In Tom's case you can add a love of food. However, to be fair, as I look around at fellow patrons at the grocery store today, I'm not so sure that Down's folks have any corner on the obesity market. Tom's physique did change over the years (like mine hasn't?). From a wiry little kid he began the transformation to the middle-aged Michelin Man's understudy. That is to say Tom's exercise and eating program did not exactly pave the way for a leaner and meaner America.

Like most of us, when Tom hit about forty, he started packing on more pounds than a couple of lines of bowling a week could remove. It seems Mom was always letting his pants out a little when he came home for a visit. With his bald head (and I mean bald—no beard, mustache, eyebrows, or eye lashes), his ability to sit in the lotus position for hours, and his growing rotundity, he began to take on the proportions and aura of a Buddha. If he were allowed to go around the house bare-chested, people would have been laying offerings in front of him.

Going around the house without a shirt on was not Tom's style though (nor his mother's). Tom had no problem with nudity but it was predominantly reserved for the bathroom or the bedroom. He could be standing there pasty-white and stark naked after a bath, maybe dangling the towel he had used to dry with, and not have a care who dropped by for a visit. The same thing happened when he used the toilet. There was no need to close the door. Ever. We could be having a nice party going on in the living room when Tom would need to make a trip to the Loo. After receiving permission, he'd quietly gather a couple of magazines and then head off on his mission. We'd usually realize, a little too late (after that sustained, low E-flatulent note), that the bathroom door, which looks right out on the living room of my parent's house, was fully ajar. Simultaneously several of us would call out, "Tom, close the door!" Usually it was too late for him to close the door as he had already planted himself on the seat and had begun perusing the reading material he had meticulously picked out. A family member would quickly volunteer to close the door for him.

Tom would normally greet the door closer with his classic, "Hey, hey, hey Bub!" to indicate that everything was just fine with him. When Tom returned, if he returned (he could sit forever, if allowed), there was never a hint of embarrassment. He was just pleased that all systems were go.

Although Tom was developing portly proportions, this did not mean that all of his personal appearance was downgrading. To the contrary. Tom took great care in his wardrobe and how he arranged each article of clothing.

First, everything was to be folded two or three times until it was just right. This included freshly laundered clothes as well as clothes that were in need of laundering. Just because a shirt had been worn for a day didn't mean that it didn't have rights and that it did not deserve the same consideration as a clean garment.

Second, belts were not necessarily meant to go through each belt loop. If it happened to miss a couple of loops, there was no penalty, as long as it passed through at least one.

Third, garments were meant to be tucked into something. Shirttails were not meant to be flying in the breeze. No! They were to be smartly tucked into your underpants with the elastic and perhaps two to three inches of white cotton brief to be clearly visible above the waist of your trousers. This tucking rule had a corollary for socks as well. Trouser legs were not to be sloppily flapping about like so many of today's fashionistas purport in their slick magazines. Tom's fashion rules clearly stated that, "All pant legs shall be snuggly tucked into the sock of which each foot and leg belong. No exemptions." Mom and Dad were continually trying to meddle with this rule by pulling out his pant cuffs from his socks, stuffing his shirttail between his undershorts and pants, and rethreading his belt. But come the next morning or his return from the bathroom, some or all of his rules would be re-established.

Tying shoes and buttoning buttons were a little out of Tom's dexterity range but he managed everything else pretty well. He also still loved to get dressed up, so having Dad knot his neck-tie and help him slip into a sport coat was a big deal. Tom did not go to church in jeans. No way! Not even in the twenty-first century when it seems like you can get away with dressing in cut-offs and a sweatshirt.

CHAPTER 9

Food

"Just a spoon full of sugar makes
The medicine go down."

—Mary Poppins

Tom had an awful addiction to sugar.

He wasn't alone. I still have this addiction and confess that after a good workout at the gym I have been known to congratulate myself with a quart of chocolate milk and a Snickers Bar. The net calorie loss from my five mile run is absolutely crushed by my sports drink and healthy snack.

I'll blame my mom but I know she'll just turn around and blame hers. Grandma will blame her mother. And so it will go for generation after generation until if finally ends up in the Garden of Eden with Eve innocently mainlining Hostess brand HoHos while getting Adam to do Twinkies.

I mentioned Tom's and my quest for sugar when we were younger. We went to great heights, literally, to get our sugar high. It seemed like there was always something to be had in and around the kitchen. Stuff like cookies, cake, Kool-aide, candy, graham crackers, and 'mallows. As I got older and understood the value of a dollar, I also discovered the corner store at the end of the block that could supply me with additional empty calories and start me down the road to elevated triglycerides should I start to run a little deficient. I'm convinced the only thing that kept me from childhood obesity was the fact that my friends and I ran around everywhere and played outdoors for twenty hours a day. It must have been an act of grace that kept Tom relatively trim, along with ten hours of dancing a day.

If it sounds like Mom fed us nothing but sugar, it's not true. Elsie Jansen graduated from Iowa State University (then College) with a degree in Home Economics and knew what a balanced meal was and how to serve it. She did a great job of providing us with wonderful opportunities to eat balanced meals. Mom also tended to fix lots of desserts. I cannot remember a single dinner meal without something sweet to finish. If dessert was not on the official curriculum at Iowa State College in the 1940s, it was definitely part of the course in the Jansen-Rechsteiner household where Mom grew up. Mom, at ninety-two, still believes in the power of sugar. No meal, including breakfast, is really complete without something laced with white sugar. Cold cereal is a failure unless it has been heaped with three or four spoonfuls of granulated sugar. If it doesn't resemble the Swiss Alps in winter, there simply isn't enough sugar on it. Filled candy dishes are also still an important part of their home décor. If ever I need a candy bar, a Good-n-Plenty, an M&M (like you can eat just one), a Bit-O-Honey, or any other type of small candy, what Mom sometimes refers to as "crazies," I'm only a five minute walk away.

Tom, me, and my sister made valiant attempts to eat Mom's balanced offerings unless they might have involved peas, green beans, Brussels sprouts, cabbage, tomatoes, liver, squash, lima beans, spinach, or skim milk, to name a few. On the other hand, Jeff had a broad palate and would eat anything put in front of him. His classic ploy was to always order pizza with anchovies. While the rest of us were studiously trying to remove every vestige of those caterpillars or eyebrows or whatever they were, Jeff was snorking down two-thirds of the pie. Then he'd taunt us the whole time that he was going to breathe anchovy breath on us. Unfortunately Tom, Nancy, and I were picky eaters at the time. Nancy may still hide her peas under the lip of her dinner plate, I'm not sure. Nonetheless, we grew up in the era of strict disciplinary food police and we were forced to eat at least some of each food on our plate that we didn't like. This cruel and inhumane treatment was exacerbated by a torturous constraint system known as captain's chairs. Each of the six dining room chairs had arms, and when the chair was pushed up closely to the table there was no way to slip out of its shackles. You were trapped until you received permission to push your chair away.

On occasion, there would be epic battles of willpower at the dinner table, often initiated when a parental unit would say, "You need to eat that tomato slice or there will be no dessert." Or, "You'll have to try six peas before you can go out and play."

"I can't stand tomatoes. They make me want to throw up!"

"One slice and you can go out to play."

"How about three peas instead?"

Back and forth negotiations would go. My sister was the best negotiator and usually obtained her freedom through overt whining or surreptitiously feeding the cat under the table (although technically I don't think feeding the cat actually counted as negotiating). After an eternity (five minutes maybe), I would finally gag down a miniscule tomato molecule, choking and trying to subdue urges to regurgitate.

On the other side of the table, Tom just sat there, easily outlasting the opposition. He was willing to wait until the next day, if necessary, to get out of eating a hunk of liver. He had superhuman nerve endings and could sit for hours without any sign of discomfort. Then for added spite, he'd pick up a napkin and start dangling it for entertainment.

"Hello? Am I being punished here?"

The problem was that we had developed a sophisticated taste (addiction) for sweet and fatty things while ignoring yucky tasting things called healthy food. Over the years, I think we all finally outgrew ignoring yucky stuff (except Brussels sprouts), but none of us have ever gotten beyond feeding the lust for more sugar. Pre-Novocain era trips to the dentist every six months were dreaded events because we knew that Dr. Hudak would always find at least three cavities. He would then gleefully attack these decaying teeth with his ultra-slow speed, "TortureMatic," drill, the bit of which he had intentionally dulled on the patient just before me. I can still smell the pungent odor of burning decayed tooth wafting to my nostrils while trying to scream--muffled only by two sets of hands and a hamster-powered, belt-drive drill working in my mouth. It still gives me the heebie-jeebies.

Tom's attitude about food rapidly changed after going to Rome State School. I think his first class was Power Eating 101. The class description and syllabus would have looked like this:

- Learn to eat rapidly. Here at Rome State there are five thousand mouths to feed, not including staff. A leisurely meal over candle-light is not a part of the program. Techniques for shoveling food will be explored.
- Develop a personal food defense initiative. Food can be a scarce commodity, and foreign forks may find their way to your plate if improper defense barriers are not established. Learn effective hoarding and shielding

strategies against those who have an eye on anything that might be construed as unattended on your plate.
- Seize opportunities for additional personal growth. Test theories of Social Darwinism, right at your own table. A neighbor's weak defensive game may be just the opportunity you need to increase your calorie count for the day. A practicum using the "direct grab" and the "stealthy snitch" methods will be employed in this laboratory setting.
- Grades will be assigned based on your weight gain (or loss) over the semester.

After Tom's first semester, he was a changed man. Pickiness was no longer in his vocabulary. If it was on his plate, it was consumed, and with great haste.

Eating speed was now paramount. Tom was slow in almost everything in life except eating. He was typically meticulous and careful and took life at a pedestrian pace. However, after completing Power Eating 101, food disappeared almost instantly. In pre-Rome days, Tom was often fed first at our table. In post-Rome days if he was served first, he'd be ready for seconds before the last person had even been given their initial offering.

Food that lollygagged around on your plate was not safe if you sat next to Tom. If you took your eyes off your plate for a moment, it was subject to being reallocated to Tom's plate, or more accurately, his palate. Tom perfected the two finger snitch and it happened so deftly and quietly that you often never knew what had struck. One minute you had a piece of chicken on your plate, the next, it had vanished. There were parental measures taken to correct some of these behaviors, but his propensity to purloin your sirloin never completely abated. If you caught him in the act, he'd start scolding himself with "No! No! No!" prior to breaking into an infectious giggle. This rapid transition from mea culpa to the joyful and righteous redeemed tended to cast doubt on the true penitence of his confession. In any event, there was already a bite out of your stolen drumstick, so what could you do?

This was not a laughing matter, entirely. Tom's habit of stealing food off of your plate was a concern that frequently needed to be addressed. A stern scolding from the victim or sometimes a flick on the ear from Dad might be meted out as punishment. He would usually respond appropriately with a little remorse but by the next meal the temptation would return. The only time I can remember yelling at Tom in anger is when he would steal my food. This was a bad habit he was never able to break.

The only time that I saw Tom refuse food (after Rome) was when my brother tried to make a cherry pie that ended up being inedible by anyone's standards. Jeff was probably trying to get a Boy Scout merit badge at the time and didn't quite make the distinction between a lightly mixed dough and a dough mixed with an electric beater. The piecrust wasn't a total loss in that Jeff did discover the recipe for an early form of Kevlar body armor. As for creating an edible food substance, well, his venture came up short. Tom not only didn't eat it, but he couldn't eat it and that was an incredible frustration for a new member of the clean plate club. I remember Tom being in tears in that there was something that still looked like food remaining on his plate that couldn't even be gagged down. Jeff now bakes cakes and leaves the pies to professionals.

One of Tom's favorite foods was pancakes. They were often categorized as one word, "pancakewaffle," which meant either a pancake or a waffle, or maybe even French toast. Basically something that provided an adequate surface area onto which one could slather butter and drown in syrup. Tom's favorite thing to order at Perkins restaurant was pancakes. It did not matter if it was breakfast time, lunch, or dinner. If you were at Perkins it had to be pancakes. If you also ordered them and you happened to sit next to "Sticky Fingers," extra vigilance was required. A tall stack might instantly become a short stack if you weren't on your best defensive game.

While living in Ames, Tom would often come home on Friday night or Saturday morning and go back to his house after Sunday dinner. Every Saturday night, without exception, Tom would start lobbying Mom regarding the menu offering for Sunday morning.

"PPPPPPancakewaffle...mornin'," he'd firmly state.

Mom would kindly reassure him that pancakes were in his future. However, just to be sure, he'd ask again about ten minutes later.

"PPPPPPancakewaffle...mornin'!"

"Yes, Tom, we'll have pancakes in the morning."

On through the evening hours the same question would pop up regularly until he was finally tucked snuggly in bed, prayers said and the lights turned out. Quietly, Mom would retreat from his bedroom, open the door to leave, only to hear one last time,

"PPPPPPancakewaffle...mornin'."

Sometimes, just to keep everyone on their toes, he would request, "Oatmeal-egg."

When morning light began to break, Tom would be right back at it. Only now he substituted coffee for waffle, so the question/request/demand became, "Pancake-coffee." When shopping for groceries with Mom, Tom also seemed to know the frozen food aisle pretty well as he would predictably stop in front of the Eggo frozen waffle section. This led me to believe that frozen waffles was a staple at his weekday home. I can only conject that syrup was bought in gallon containers.

Tom's love of pancakes (and syrup) nearly bought him a trip to the emergency room when the folks lived in Spokane, Washington.

Nancy and I had been working in the mountains just east of Spokane all summer preparing building materials to be used for the construction of foot bridges and out-door shelters for an Environmental Educational Center being developed by Whitworth College. It was known as the Ragged Ridge Environmental Center and Dad was its first director. Along with a host of regional educators and naturalists, they mapped out an extensive experiential learning complex to be used by local school districts in an attempt to relate environmental issues with core academic studies. Nancy and I spent our college summer break helping out. Our days would usually start with loading up our Volkswagen Beetle with a couple of axes, a chain saw, gas, and bar oil before making the forty minute drive to the forest where we cut and peeled Tamarac trees and then dispersed them to the various building sites for later construction.

One weekend, while Tommy was visiting from his Medical Lake residential facility, mischief was in the air. For some forgotten reason the folks needed to run an errand with Tom. The VW was already parked in the drive-way so they put Tom in the back seat as they headed to town. Everything was normal and quiet in the car. Tom began to giggle a little from the back seat, but not enough to raise suspicions from the front. Another giggle, then a generous belch. Moments later the smell of motor oil began to waft up to the driver's seat. Another burp, more giggles, more motor oil fumes, then the telltale, "No! No! No!" Something was up! Mom turned around from the passenger's seat and there was the Buddha of Pennzoil sitting cross-legged holding onto an Aunt Jemima syrup bottle that I had been using as a chainsaw bar-oil dispenser. He had taken the container out of the box next to him on the back seat and somehow unsecured the child-proof lid and was contentedly self-lubricating with my bar-oil, thinking that somewhere in that plastic squeeze bottle maple syrup could be found.

Mom and Dad quickly pulled into the next service station and called the hospital. Their advice was to get him home, feed him several slices of bread and give him lots of water. Then keep a careful eye on him. More than likely all will harmlessly pass. As it ended up, Tom was fine. However, we were informed that there was an epic bowel movement the next day replete with its own oil slick.

From that day forward, chainsaw equipment was religiously stowed in the trunk. There was also a wake-up call that sounded. It reminded us all that Tom did have limitations and that we needed to keep a sharper eye-out for him. When you live with person with a disability, it's easy to get accustomed to their actions such that you may become a little lazy with what they can and can't do. We had all forgotten that Tom's ability to discern real danger or make correct choices functioned in a diminished capacity.

CHAPTER 10

Picking up Chicks

"Did you happen to see the most beautiful girl in the world?
And if you did, was she crying, crying..."
>   —Johnny Mathis, "The Most Beautiful Girl in the World"

This will be a short chapter. Tom didn't pick up chicks, they picked him up. Just that simple.

So you're wondering what his secret was, the magic spell he'd put on the ladies so they'd approach him? Wouldn't you like to know? Wouldn't I like to know!

The brief answer is, I don't know. Once he began to lose his hair, then teeth, then pick up too many pounds, this cute cherubic little guy began to look like a relative of Jabba the Hut minus the warts and pointy tongue. Sorry Tom, that's a little over the top. He began to look like an understudy to the Pillsbury Doughboy (there, is that better? Jealous? Who me?).

So here you have this bald, toothless, overweight, cross-eyed, bespeckled dumpling with girls fawning over him like he was Justin Timberlake. What's the deal?

We'd go to the outdoor band concert in the summer down at the local park and this parade of women would come by.

"Oh, hi Tom! How's it going?"

Tom would get out of his lawn chair, make complete eye contact with his brow-less, lash-less blue eyes, and reach out his hand to just simply touch the lady's hand. Next thing you know, she's over with her arm around his shoulder kissing the top of his head while he leans into her.

Standing up, I'd puff out my chest a little and introduce myself, "Hi, I'm Steve, Tom's brother."

Somewhat stiffly she'd reply, "Nice to meet you."

Along comes another lady, one of the college attendants down at his group home. "TOM!" she squeals as she runs up and gives him a bear hug. I mean, she can't even get her hands to link up behind him because of his generous girth. She holds him for a couple of seconds then steps back. He makes gentle eye contact.

"Hey, hey, hey Bub," is all he has to say.

She turns into a puddle of putty. He gets another kiss.

"Hi, I'm Steve, Tom's brother," I try to say in a suave, smooth baritone.

Another curt, "Hi, I'm Jennifer."

Yet another comely lady spots Tom from halfway across the crowded park and starts on a sprint. Out of breath, she makes eye contact with Mr. Studly T. Muffin.

"Hey Tom. I missed you at the workshop on Tuesday. Are you okay?"

After putting her into his spell with these caring, searching eyes, she takes his hand in hers and they just kind of stand there. Hand in hand. Tom coyly wags his head back and forth a few times, obviously enjoying the moment. "Sssssmmaaaack!" Another tender kiss on his cheek. I nudge him to kindly introduce me to his groupie. All I get back is an insipid toothless smile that says without words, "Get your own friends, bro."

"Hello, I'm Tom's brother, Steve." I try again.

"Don't you just love this guy?" she says in a far-away voice. "I mean, what's it like being his brother and everything?"

The concert starts and this despicable public display of affection finally stops.

Tom set his sights high, and even for him there were some women that were out of his league. However, that is probably only because of geography or the fact that some of his ladies were TV personalities who he knew only as phosphorescent pixels on a screen. He had the hots for Norma Zimmer of the Lawrence Welk show for over forty-five years. She'd show up, her whole face filling the TV screen, and croon some song through the brightest, whitest set of teeth since Pepsodent stopped protecting our teeth with jet-age plastic. Tom would point at the TV and say, "Noohma, Noohma!" If we did not acknowledge that we too saw Norma, we'd be told all over again. I'm sure that if Norma and Tom had ever met in person, she would have been helpless under his magic too.

Soon after we moved to Chappaqua, New York, in 1967, Tom was down on a visit from Rome and shopping for groceries with Mom at the local A&P. Then all of a sudden, right there in the produce section, was Lorraine 'Lolo' Lemieux, temptress, sexpot, and home wrecker on the ever popular soap opera, *As the Stomach Wretches*. It seems that Chappaqua, being only a fifty minute commute from Manhattan, was home to several actors and actresses who worked out of New York studios. Of course, the Soap Opera starlet was not in costume or character and not made-up as she pushed her cart through the store. With his eagle eye, though, Tom recognized this woman and went up to her pointing at her and calling her by her stage name.

The stunned actress was taken back initially until Mom explained the situation. There was a good laugh shared and he probably got a hug and a kiss out of that encounter too. Disgusting!

My wife was another casualty of his amorous mojo. These two couldn't stop hugging when they'd see each other when we'd go over to the folks' house to visit or share a meal while Tom was home.

"He's so soft and cushy. He's just great to squeeze," she'd say. (I think there may have been an inference in that statement that maybe I was a little crunchy to squeeze, but I'm not sure.)

Anyway, they'd sit down on the couch next to each other, Tom giving his adoring eye look and his coy little mutterings while my wife, Dot, had her arms around his shoulders. Then a little peck on the cheek.

"Break it up you two!" Mom would finally scold from across the room. "It's time for dinner."

Break it up indeed!

I tried studying Tom's moves, his style, his savoir faire. He obviously had something going for him that I didn't and I thought that maybe if I went about studying him scientifically, I might be able to share with men everywhere the results of my research and perhaps, the betterment of mankind. The following is what I observed. It may be formulaic, but in Tom's hands it never failed. Guys, take note and good luck.

- When a woman enters the room, you don't have to jump to your feet. You can remain a little cool and distant, doing what you had been doing all along—maybe reading a magazine cross legged on the floor or dangling a cloth.
- When said woman is within your gravitational influence, stand and look her gently in the eye with a look that says, "You're the most beautiful thing I have ever

seen." Don't speak. Just look. Look at one eye then the other. Repeat three or four times. Don't break eye contact even though it might seem uncomfortable. Go with the gentle love-fest look.

- When your subject begins to smile awkwardly, then you smile too. It helps if you don't have any teeth and you can crinkle your eyes up to where they disappear between your eyebrow (or where your eyebrow should be) and your cheeks.
- Gently extend a forefinger and thumb out toward the target woman and tap them together (finger-tip to thumb-tip) rapidly about five or six times while you say, "Hey, hey, hey Bub" (you can substitute their real name if you know it). The other fingers (middle through baby finger) should be loosely extended (not clenched). Practice an hour or so every day.
- At this point, the woman will be melting and will put her arm around your shoulder. Don't hug back. Your next move is, with your arms at your side, to simply lean your head so that your forehead touches her shoulder.
- Her second arm will now wrap around you.
- Game over.

There is little doubt that Tom was smooth with the ladies.

What was he thinking? Perhaps the better question is, what was he feeling? What kind of comprehension of human sexuality did he have? Was he attracted to the opposite sex for the same reasons I am? How did he process the issues of puberty and maturing to adulthood? Does the need for a mate transcend mental capability? How does a person with a severe disability...

...Hey, don't look at me for those answers. Do I look like an expert?

CHAPTER 11

Mama!Papa!

"Where are we going, Tom?" I'd ask as I opened the door to the car to take him to the folk's house for a weekend visit.

"Mama!Papa!" (one word) Tom would emphatically say, pushing the tip of his index finger into the palm of his other hand to make sure I didn't miss the point. We were going to Mom and Dad's house! This is the world of music, puzzles, pancakes, pop, candy bars, music, and love. This is the place that Tom knew for almost sixty years, with its routines as constant as the setting and rising of the sun.

Mama!Papa! was Tom's wonderland; sanctuary; his nirvana. The 'Mama' part was really the key ingredient to this special world. Although Dad provided wisdom, economic stability, discipline, insight into great truths, engineering insights, chore lists, and hands-on training such as to how to hammer a nail (from the elbow dammit, not the wrist), and appreciated and encouraged us all, it was Mom who created a well nurtured center at the heart of the household.

Elsie Jansen and Merle Prater met at a dance mixer at Iowa State College in the fall of 1942, where they were students during World War II. Dad obtained a degree in electrical engineering while in the U.S. Naval Officer Program and Mom graduated with a degree in home economics.

In 1944, Mom graduated and then taught home economics until they were married. After that she did some clerical work as she followed Dad while the Navy shuffled him from Iowa to New York to Boston to San Diego to Los Angeles before getting his ship assignment in late August 1945. Dad was a communication officer on a troop transport ostensibly planned for delivering soldiers to the shores of Japan for the imminent invasion that would include nearly a million U.S. fighting forces. Two words scuttled the invasion: Hiroshima and Nagasaki or if you prefer, atomic bombs. Dad's mission changed overnight from delivery to retrieval. His ship was now directed to pick up troops that had been scattered around the far reaches of the South Pacific and bring them home. He was discharged from the Navy in 1946 in Boston when his ship was unceremoniously decommissioned.

While on the East Coast, Dad decided to follow up on a job contact he had made years earlier with a little upstart business machine company in upstate New York. International Business Machines (IBM) was just getting into main-frame computing and took a gamble on hiring about twenty engineers as part of a long-range expansion plan. Dad was in that class. He and Mom settled into the Triple Cities area of the rolling hills of South Central New York.

With a solid job and the confidence that the civilized world might survive, the folks thought it time to start a family. Dad's engineering salary was enough for Mom to stay at home once children started coming along in 1947. Although she had credentials to teach, she opted to stay at home to nurture and manage us kids, along with a host of other domestic responsibilities.

However, Mom didn't completely leave the workforce. From time to time she would answer the call to be a substitute teacher in home economics at the junior or senior high school. The phone would ring early in the morning and the rest of us usually knew what that meant. Mom would be working today. When she consented to teach, the whole household would shift into panic mode and everything seemed to be thrown into frantic chaos. I'd be given lunch money instead of a packed sandwich. I wouldn't bother to comb my hair or brush my teeth and it would go unchecked. My tee shirt might be on inside out and backwards (my unofficial name badge for the day: "Fruit of the Loom") and I'd probably forget my band instrument. It frazzled Mom more than a little to transform from home-maker to school teacher in a matter of minutes. I think she was much more comfortable as a home-maker than a home economist anyway. Somehow, I can't envision her scribbling organic chemistry equations on a black board indicating the proper time to take an egg out of boiling water to obtain its maximum nutrition. Making a home is where she excelled and she made a place for all us kids and Dad to grow, explore, speak our minds (within civil boundaries), and take risks.

Our home was a safe and comfortable place where friends and neighbors were welcomed and a household where I remember a lot of laughter. Mom's speaking voice is relatively low pitched and sonorous and she has this little guttural chuckle that usually begins or ends whatever it is that she is saying. It is one of those pleasant, babbling brook type sounds that makes you feel that everything is good and that this lady can be trusted with anything. She herself could get worried and nervous but when she spoke it seemed to make dire situations seem like they were just little clouds passing by and the sun would soon follow. Even in the midst of a terrible trial, she'd quote "This too shall pass," and say it in such a non-condescending tone that it provided comfort rather than just being an idle platitude.

I remember little nagging or arguing or just plain bitchy vibes. We weren't scolded often for letting the screen door bang shut or for leaving the front door wide open. There were the usual reminders to turn off the lights when we weren't using them and to flush the toilet, but for just plain annoying kid stuff there was rarely a rebuke. I could be practicing fielding ground balls by throwing a rubber ball at the wooden steps for twenty minutes or working on pop flies by catching a ball returning to earth via a bounce or two off the roof with about 99% immunity. For a while, I relished jumping down the final flight of steps from the landing to the living room floor rather than taking each step one at a time. The house shook when I thumped to a landing, but so long as I didn't break myself or the house, it was okay.

Mom was not a great disciplinarian. Even though she had a pretty full trunk-load of German and Swiss genetic material, Mom was not constantly correcting or disciplining us for minor infractions. The worst penalty was to hear the words, "Wait until your father gets home!" That was usually the signal to shape up big time in hopes that Mom would forget about the incident before Dad's arrival from work. If she remembered, there was a solid chance of corporal punishment to be expected, but there were equal odds that she'd forget. On a couple of occasions when pushed beyond the breaking point, Mom came after me with a fly swatter raised in retribution. Running away from her was somehow allowed and almost part of the sport. I can remember one time being chased around the dinner table, then upstairs, where I dove under my bed with a wildly flaying fly swatter just nano-seconds behind me, grazing me but inflicting no real damage. I wouldn't have thought about doing that with Dad.

Did I get away with murder? Probably not *murder*, but certainly many misdemeanors. I don't think that the discipline in our household was what would be termed "permissive", but it may have edged to the lenient side. Dad had a firmer disciplinarian's hand so that between the two of them I think we got the necessary guidance we needed. When Dot and I started raising our children, I found out that I favored my mother's leniency and had to get some remedial help. I admit that I have not been the best at setting and defending parental boundaries and that too often that responsibility has fallen on my wife's shoulders.

I know, I'll blame Tom for my poor performance as a disciplinarian!

Seriously, Tom probably did have an impact on how discipline was administered. He seemed to be a happy and contented guy almost all of the time. This is one of the most wonderful traits of most Down syndrome people (there are some cantankerous Down's persons, but they tend to be a minority). This gentle demeanor was an early and regular observation of those pioneering the formal study and care of this special branch of humanity. Words like "blithe," "happy," and "content" are used regularly in descriptions. The great thing is that no matter how normal society treats them or tries to heal them of their infirmity, they seem to keep popping up to the surface like joyful corks. Perhaps some of Tom's perpetual geniality rubbed-off on our family members.

Tom rarely got disciplined (probably because he didn't need it) but if he started snitching food from someone's plate, Dad might flick Tom's ear with his finger. Tom's response was a very vocal and prolonged, "OOOOWWWW!" If it didn't hurt that much, he made it sound like it did.

I'm sure punishment for a lot of my indiscretions as a kid were tempered by having such a compliant and empathetic colleague. On occasions when he witnessed me get swatted or spanked, he'd even cry and say "Ow" right along with me.

Discipline is not always about correcting negative behavior, though. It is also about establishing good habits like learning to do chores, listening to others and encouraging others to explore and develop their latent gifts. Along with making sure we all had daily chores, Mom also made sure that we were adequately exposed to the arts. Her thinking was that the arts were not just meant to be appreciated, but to be participated in. We all took piano, played instruments and sang in choirs. Jeff and Nancy went on to formally study music and became professional musicians. I have sung several arias accompanied by running shower water, where I do my best work. With my musical talent, such as it was, I went into the visual arts, ending up as an architect for thirty years. But my parents encouraged that as well. I vividly remember one of my favorite Christmas presents was a full-size wooden oil-paint box, filled with regular sized tubes of oil-paint and a collapsible aluminum easel. Another gift was a small drafting table with all of the equipment necessary to make measured drawings. Both are still in active use fifty years later.

Even Tom was not excused from learning how to perform. When home for visits, Mom and Tom would sit down on the piano bench together to belt out a few classic duets. Mom would accompany herself to a familiar tune and then on the last syllable of the phrase or line pause for Tom to chime in the missing word. She treated him like a rock star, always giving him the punch line. A song might go as follows:

Mom: "Frosty the snow..."
    ...Pause...
Tom: "Man"
Mom: "Was as happy as can..."
    ...Pause...
Tom: "Be"

And so on until they had made it through the entire song. Then another song, and then another. They had a repertoire of maybe five or six songs, but each was sung with the same enthusiasm time after time, day after day, year after year. Each had a half measure's rest before Tom's climactic final vocal interjection. Without a deep bond of love, this ritual and daily engagement would have tried the patience of the holiest of saints. There was a certain magic between those two at the piano bench that can't be explained by logic.

Around holidays we'd invariably all make music together on our instruments around the piano. The key signature needed to be carefully selected to match one of two keys that Dad's harmonica could play in. Then we'd all join in, blasting our lungs out on our school instruments: Jeff on trombone, Nancy on the French horn, and me on a tarnished baritone I rarely practiced. Tom held the rhythm section down with maracas, tambourine, or whatever other percussive instrument was laying around. He couldn't hold a beat but we could barely hear him over the din we were creating anyway. Mom tried to keep us together with her singing and piano playing while trying to direct us with her head wagging. We usually ended pretty much together but the quality of sound probably came out more like a front-end loader pushing a load of scrap steel into a landfill. No matter. As beauty is in the eye of the beholder, our music was ecstasy in the ear of the tone deaf. Making music at home was not about performing a concert anyway, it was about doing something constructive together. In modern psycho-babel, it would be defined as a cooperative venture in family dynamics whereby each family unit may extract rich veins of precious self-esteem and personal satisfaction. For us, it was just fun. Until just a couple of years ago we still held to this tradition at Christmas time. Family and friends were asked to bring their musical instruments along and then after dinner we'd hunker around the piano playing carols. Those without instruments were assigned to the choir.

Speaking of satisfaction, Mom was and still is a great baker (that home-ec degree paid some big dividends) and the cookie jar was rarely empty. It seemed that the kitchen table with a cookie and milk was always the first stop after school before moving outdoors with friends.

Holiday baking was always a high priority and the smells drove the rest of us crazy. Jeff, Tom, Nancy, and I were usually not far away to provide TQM (total quality management) services for product moving through the kitchen. Decorating sugar cut-out cookies were our specialty. Unfortunately, many finished cookies never passed muster and required instant (and surreptitious) removal from the production line. We were ruthless about culling unsuitable cookies (when Mom's back was turned) and making sure that inferior goods would not sully Mother's fine reputation.

> Mom: "Hey, I thought I had a dozen cookies on this cooling rack." Looking at us, "Did somebody here snitch one?"

> Tom: With cookie crumbs on his lips, squeal, giggle, giggle, "No!No!No!"

> Jeff, Steve, and Nan: With cookie crumbs on their lips, shrugged shoulders.

> Outcome: A token scolding with Tom taking most of the rap and forty fingers perched in readiness to nab another cookie given the right opportunity.

From Halloween through the end of December, we bravely shouldered through a dangerously high-sugar environment. If there were Geiger counters that could register sugar content, ours would have been making a solid hum.

Everything was not always sugar coated, though, and there was occasional discord in the house. Especially as our parents got into their late seventies and eighties, disagreements started cropping up more often between them. I don't remember many arguments growing up, but as Mom and Dad's hearing started deteriorating, body parts losing full function, and vision dimmed, perhaps it was too easy to let impatience get the upper hand. When Tom was home, though, he would have no part of these emotional exchanges. If Mom or Dad started getting a little snippy with each other, Tom would clap his hands loudly a time or two as if to say, "Enough, you two. Now let's get along with each other!" For better or for worse, his response is a page out of my mom's playbook, which stated that, "Getting along with each other is paramount to just about everything else." A heated argument in Mom's presence was rarely allowed. Tom also found that being in the company of people not in agreement was very uncomfortable for him.

Tom did not like contentious situations. He learned some of that at home, but I believe it is also a relatively familiar trait found in a large part of the Down's community. Loud arguing or heated discussion can be upsetting and intimidating for almost everyone. Because rapid verbal expression is not a hallmark of persons with Down syndrome, it must be overwhelming when it happens, leaving them feeling vulnerable. With a diminished capacity for quick analytical thinking and rapid rejoinders, entering into an argument with a fully functioning person is usually out of the question. If Tom ever took a dissenting position or had an opinion that was over-ruled, his typical form of debate would be to employ passive obstinacy.

I have not personally witnessed exactly how disputes are settled or hierarchy established within the Down's community itself. I presume that there is some positioning to establish a little pecking order but I know it is not nearly of the magnitude most of us are used to in normal circles.

I believe Tom's non-argumentative behavior influenced how I function too. I don't avoid all confrontations, but I do make serious attempts to mollify conditions where a possible conflict might arise. I also feel unconfident in verbal sparring. I can easily discuss, but when I feel myself being drawn into an impassioned argument my face flushes, I get short of breath, and my analytical reasoning skills seem to vanish into thin air. I'm liable to lose the simplest of debates, so don't look for me to run for political office.

I can't say for sure that having my earliest playmate be so docile was the reason for my lack of arguing skills, but I sometimes wonder if it made a significant contribution. The childhood tit-for-tat, fighting over toys, or elbowing for position was pretty much missing as Tom was so willing to give me whatever I asked for. Jeff provided some sibling rivalry but he was four years older and could easily out maneuver me in most contests of brain and brawn.

The ability to remain calm and stem argumentative situations has usually served me well. However, there have been instances where I have shied away from occasions that needed to be dealt with more directly and perhaps emotionally.

Now, where can I go to practice that hand clap Tom used so effectively?

CHAPTER 12

Blessed are the Meek

"Blessed are the meek,
for they shall inherit the earth."

Matthew 5:5

When we all get to heaven, and I am certain we all will (at least to the screening desk), we're in for a rude awakening. I have it on good authority that the first question at the check-in counter is going to be, "Do you like Lawrence Welk?"

If you answer, yes and you don't even know who Lawrence Welk is, you are just digging yourself into a deeper hole because the follow-up question is, "Who is Myron Floren, and what instrument does he play?"

If you don't like accordion music (sorry, no exceptions here) you're screwed because you certainly won't know the answer to, who is Bobby's dance partner? ("Sissy," you knucklehead!)

For five hundred points, who do you think will be at the main gate asking these questions? Saint Peter?

Wrong again. It will be one of the gentle people who we mostly ignored in our life who may have had Down syndrome, been autistic, or had some other condition that caused them to have a mental deficiency (by our definition). They will now be running everything. The big switch is that for eternity we're going to have to play by the rules that these folks knew all along. They won't be the disadvantaged ones any more. It will be the rest of us needing remedial help, and we'd better start learning to like Lawrence Welk-style champagne bubble music, pronto.

I don't want to be a prophet of doom, but if you don't dance, and I don't mean like the tango or other complicated dances, I mean like rocking back and forth (maybe a little twisting or some quasi-disco) for hours on end, you'd better go out and buy the best arch supports money can buy and start practicing. You do not need to worry if you're jiven' to the beat or keeping time to the music or looking like the hottest thing on the dance floor. You don't need costumes with shirts that are open to your waist, nor skirts that are slit to your armpits. High-heels, gold chains, and slick hair are not required. You just need to move and keep moving. Otherwise, I'm afraid you're going to think you're in hell.

Also, if you've practiced deceit and conceit and scratched your way to the top at other peoples' expense, I'm sorry to inform you that those values will not be useful anymore either. I urge you to go to a Special Olympics game near you for re-schooling. I think almost every state in the country has one. Observe what true sportsmanship is all about and what it means to really compete.

The Special Olympics was the outgrowth of a personal encounter that the Kennedys had with mental retardation in their own family. Rosemary, one of the children that Joseph and Rose Kennedy raised, had a mental disability. During their political years, Jack, Robert, and Ted did a great deal to advance public policy toward persons with disabilities, but their sister Eunice became directly involved with trying to advance living and life conditions for people with physical or intellectual limitations.[21] Starting in the mid-1950s, she helped established camps for mentally or physically challenged citizens. These camps, which began to multiply across the country, tended to have a strong component of physical activity and game playing. As an outgrowth of their popularity, the first Special Olympics was held in Chicago's Soldier Field in 1968. The idea caught on quickly and expanded to other regions of the country. Although some have criticized these organized contests for being condescending and a layering of Western societies' values on what we think they need, the participants love it. The Special Olympics has worked at bringing a lot of joy and self-respect to a huge number of developmentally disabled folks, not to mention a wonderful sense of community that spans age and intellectual abilities when these events are held.

A couple of years ago, I was watching a relay event at Iowa State University's Lied Recreational Center, where the Iowa Special Olympics is held every year. The Lied Center is a large indoor field house with basketball courts, climbing walls, exercise machines, running tracks, and everything else needed to keep today's students partially entertained and out of the library. Anyway, the Special Olympians were using it this week and it was in full swing when I stopped by. What I saw was the greatest race ever.

The relay race was going well and people were wildly cheering for their teams. It seemed like a typical American sports venue. There were eight lanes of contestants with the team members split; half at the starting line and the other half at the turn-around point about thirty-five yards away. Down and back, down and back, for four legs. The race had already started when I got there. Runners were on the second leg digging out each step with baton in hand, stretching to pass it off to the third-leg team members.

There were clean baton exchanges going into the third leg. Raucous shouting and cheering everywhere. Hands waving, clapping, kids jumping up and down. This was real fan involvement.

Runners were putting every ounce of energy into their spirited strides coming up on the final exchange of batons to their respective anchor-men.

"Oh no! A baton got dropped in lane three."

Not a problem. All the runners stopped and the guy in lane four reached down and picked up the baton and gave it back to ol' butterfingers in three.

The race resumed.

On this, the last thirty-five yard segment, when the anchor-person should have been dashing those final yards unimpeded to break the finish-line ribbon and relish in glory, something different happened. About twenty bystanders, along with the contestants who had run the first and third legs, started running the final lap right along with the eight runners who were in the race. They were met half-way by athletes who had run the second leg, as well as by another twenty or so spectators who were waiting near the finish line and just couldn't stand it anymore. The final ten yards was a melee of shouting, jubilant fans, and athletes moving amoeba-like to the finish line. Some team got medals because they had to. After all, this is America and the games were organized by folks who just have to deem a winner. But the runners and fans were just thrilled to be there, and they couldn't have been happier for the team that won—because everyone won. Although proud of the medals hanging around their necks, there was no connotation whatsoever that one athlete was better than another. There were no sore losers, no tears of dejection, no faces hidden somberly behind cupped hands, nor slumped shoulders. I got the feeling that the trophies, badges, medals, and hype were so incidental that it really didn't matter.

Can you imagine anyone thinking that a Super Bowl ring is just a trinket? Can you imagine both the Seattle Seahawks and the New England Patriots both being wildly excited after the Super Bowl for the sheer joy of having played in a game together? Can you imagine Tom Brady chest bumping with Russell Wilson and saying, "You played a great game, why don't you take the ring this year? Besides I already have one."

Russell Wilson would say, "Thanks. That's really cool. Did you like the fireworks and singing during halftime?"

Tom responds, "Oh man, that was the best part of the whole evening!"

If this doesn't sound like normal sports to you, you could find heaven a difficult place to be. Sorry, there will be no betting on sports in eternity because there won't be any clear winner.

"And the winner is... Ah, who cares?!"

"Let's party!!! Maestro Welk, strike up the band."

Several years ago, I came across an article on the internet about what things might look like if individuals with Down syndrome had control of the rules. Dr. Dennis McGuire wrote a beautiful essay entitled, *If People with Down Syndrome Ruled the World*[22]

The whole article is worthy of a careful read and you can look it up on the National Association for Down Syndrome website, but there were a couple of excerpts from his paper that really resonated. The following is verbatim from the article:

Order and Structure would rule

We have heard that many people with Down syndrome are stubborn and compulsive. Now I know what many of you are thinking... "Did you really have to bring that up?" I'm sorry, but—we do. What we hear is that quite a few people have nonsensical rituals and routines. They can get stuck on behaviors that can drive family members a little crazy.

Despite the irritations, there are also many benefits to these "obsessive compulsive tendencies." We actually have termed these tendencies "Grooves" because people tend to follow fairly set patterns, or "grooves," in their daily activities.

What are the benefits of Grooves? Many people with Down syndrome are very careful with their appearance and grooming, which is especially important since they often stand out because of their physical features. Grooves also increase independence because most people are able to complete home and work tasks reliably when these tasks are part of their daily routine. (And while they are not fast...they are very precise.) For many with Down syndrome, grooves serve as a way to relax. Some people repeat a favorite activity in a quiet space, such as writing, drawing, puzzles, needlepoint, etc. Grooves also serve as a clear and unambiguous statement of choice (very important for people with language limitations). This may even be a way for teens with Down syndrome to define their own independence without getting into the same rancorous conflicts with parents as many other teens.

So given what we know about people with Down syndrome and grooves, how would they use this to run the world? Here is how:

- *Schedules and calendars would be followed.*
- *Trains and planes would run on time.*
- *Lunch would be at 12:00. Dinner at 6:00*
- *Work time would be work time.*
- *Vacation would be vacation.*
- *People would be expected to keep their promises.*
- *Last minute changes would be strongly discouraged (if not considered rude and offensive).*
- *Places would be neat, clean, and organized (not just bedrooms, but cities, countries, the whole world.*
- *Lost and founds would go out of business (even chaotic appearing rooms have their own sense of order).*
- *The "grunge look" would be out. Way out.*

- *"Prep" (but not pretentious) would be very big.*

In the world of Down syndrome, there would be a great deal more tolerance for:

- *Repeating the same phase or question*
- *Use of the terms "fun" and "cleaning" in the same sentence.*
- *Closing doors or cabinets that are left ajar (even in someone else's house).*
- *Arranging things until they are "Just so."*

Despite their compulsions and grooves, people with Down syndrome rarely have the really 'bad habits' that so many of us have. In fact, out of approximately 3,000 people we have seen at the clinic, we have not seen any drug addicts or gamblers and just two alcoholics and a very small number of smokers. However, we think that pop may be a common addiction in the world of Down syndrome, and of course some people are incurable savers and hoarders of just about everything, but especially paper products and writing utensils. Because of this, I could see maybe a Betty Ford Center for pop addicts and extreme paper hoarding.

Dancing

- *You probably would not hear a great deal about exercise, but you may hear a phrase like, "Dancing tonight...absolutely."*
- *The President's commission on physical fitness would probably recommend dancing at least three times per week.*
- *People would be encouraged to get married several times to have more weddings for more music and dancing.*
- *Richard Simmons and John Travolta would be national heroes.*

The point of all of this is that things are going to be different. Actually, I'm a little concerned that these folks are establishing a counter-culture of contentment, here and now, and frankly I'm a little jealous of that. I think I should have a bigger slice of their pie. All right, I understand that I may have to come to like Lawrence Welk reruns on public television and resist the urge to immediately change channels, but I think I could do it. Yes, I'm sure I could! Bring on Joe Feeney, Norma Zimmer, Myron, Bobby, and Sissy and the whole gang making champagne bubbles. I am ready.

CHAPTER 13

Dodging Bullets

"O death, where is thy victory?
O death, where is thy sting?"

1 Corinthians 15:55

The Prater boys used to spend a lot of time watching Channel 12, the CBS television affiliate out of Binghamton, New York. It was the only channel our twelve inch TV would receive without an aerial two hundred feet in the air. With Dad being an electrical engineer, you would have thought that our household would have been supplied with the latest technology and that we would have at least been able to receive the NBC and ABC channels. Nope!

I'm afraid one channel is all we got until we moved just outside of the New York City area, where programs were sent from the Empire State Building and could easily be picked up in Chappaqua, thirty-five miles to the north. I guess Dad didn't want to see a big honkin' contrivance mounted to the house's chimney, and the garage already had a big honkin' fifteen meter antenna on a rotating base that Jeff used for his short wave radio. So the whole family suffered for the sake of one family member's obsession. I suppose one channel offered us enough entertainment though.

One channel notwithstanding, we still got our fill of electronic 1950s and '60s TV programming genius.

Cartoons aside, our real moral principles and ethical guidelines came from Saturday morning westerns. This is where we really learned how to identify right from wrong. It was actually pretty easy.

- If you wore a dark hat you were bad; white you were good
- If you talked mean to people and snarled, you were bad; talked nice and used a lot of "Yes Ma'am's" and "Howdy Ma'am's", you were good.
- Robbed banks or stagecoaches, bad; chased after stagecoach bandits, good.
- Shot your pistol looking backwards, bad; shot your pistol looking forwards (at the bad guys in front of you), good.

We had real role models like Hoppalong Cassidy (what parent would name their kid Hoppalong?), Sky King (Sky was an upgrade from Hoppalong but he still would have gotten beat-up on our school playground), and finally Roy Rogers, a regular name at last. More importantly, it was a name Tom could almost pronounce.

Roy Rogers and Dale Evans were always getting into some type of predicament that would involve their horse, Trigger, their dog, Bullet, and their goofy sidekick, Pat, who was always driving from one crime scene to the next in his wild-west, World War II surplus Jeep named Nellibelle. Roy and Dale would always be singing to you at the conclusion of every show: "Happy Trails to You!" Each week they both looked me right in the eye and with their crisp white hats and bandanas tied neatly around their necks they'd wish me happy trails until next week—10:00 a.m Eastern, 9:00 a.m. Central.

Most Roy Rogers shows revolved around some bad guys doing something, well, bad in Roy and Dale's neighborhood once a week. The plot was usually stealing horses or robbing a bank, or maybe robbing a horse or stealing banks. I can't think of any other plots, but I'm sure there were some that kept us coming back every Saturday morning. Roy, being the man, would figure out who the criminals were (hint: black hat) and would always chase them on horseback. The black-hat guys would also be on horseback, which I never quite understood. If Pat Brady could have a Jeep, couldn't these stage coach robbers also afford some type of motorized vehicle that could out-run Trigger? I mean, surely they could have had at least a Ford Falcon or something. Not in the Roy Roger's show they couldn't.

They'd always be riding fanatically through what appeared to be the same set week after week. Bad guys would be galloping at full speed past huge rocks, Ponderosa pines, and sage brush, kicking up clouds of dust. Meanwhile Roy and the sheriff and a few other good guys would be hot on their tails, following the humongous dust storm being whipped-up. The bad-guys would always be turned around in their saddles firing thousands of rounds out of their six-shooters that never hit Roy and his buddies. They were shooting like they were riding on animals galloping down a dusty path. Roy and the rest of the white hats would be shooting right back, having the advantage of not having to turn around in their saddles.

Roy also had another advantage and that was his horse. Trigger must have had such a smooth and steady gait while charging through the wilds of Outset 14 that his hooves never touched the ground. For Roy it must have been like riding on a magic carpet in clear air. Taking careful aim, completely unmolested by the jostling that accompanies most horseback riding, Roy would squeeze off a shot.

"POW!"

Of course he'd wound one of the members in the nasty gang. He'd fall off his horse but somehow not get trampled to death by the posse in close pursuit (nobody ever died on Roy Rogers, it wouldn't have been right). Another thousand rounds would be fired from the escaping bandit's set of second six-shooters. Bullets would be hitting something because you could hear the ricochet's taking place on the sound-track.

"Bing—zee! Bing—zee! Bing"

The ricocheting bullets would sing out after missing their intended targets and deflecting off rocks.

They'd keep up the chase until it finally dawned on Bad Black Bart that he should have robbed the bank in the next town over instead. Roy would finally wing Bart, the whole gang would instantly stop, and justice would be served. The bad guys would all get tied up and wait until Pat Brady could catch up in his Jeep and take them all back to jail where they belonged. Criminal Justice never looked so easy.

Jeff, Tom and I re-enacted these scenes in the TV room regularly with our fingers used as pistols. (Note: toy guns were not *technically* allowed in our household--at first. Over time exceptions were granted until we had quite an arsenal of cap guns, squirt guns, pop guns, toy machine guns and even plastic hand grenades.) Tom was not very good at this finger-pistol play because he had a hard time making his hand to look like a gun. He had trouble straightening his forefinger out enough and he was never able to pick up on the necessary violence that needs to accompany these actions. How do you shoot someone who looks at you, jaw a little slack, eyes crossed who all of a sudden breaks into laughter saying, "Hey, hey, hey, Bub! Hey Bub." Thank goodness Jeff and I could kill each other with a little American wild-west vigilante conviction and dignity.

Thank God those gun control radicals couldn't take our Second Amendment fingers away.

The TV gun fights were always classic events. I think Roy had a force field around him because he never got hit. With his lightening quick reflexes, you'd see him duck out of the way of an oncoming 45-caliber bullet (traveling at 3,500 feet per second) from time to time, but he'd keep right on chasing and firing. He must have dodged a million bullets in his day.

The only person who may have dodged more bullets was Tommy. His first few days of life were spent ducking, bobbing, and weaving around them.

Before Mom had hardly even left the hospital after giving birth, the medical staff suggested that she and dad leave Tom at the hospital where they would look after him. Tom, after all, could not be expected to live beyond four or five years they advised. The professionals would take good care of him. What this really meant was that if he survived his first few weeks, he would be institutionalized and left alone to live out his little life in the context of isolation and institutional abandonment.

In many cases of severe retardation or congenital physical defects, the hospital staff would refuse medical treatment and even nourishment, causing the baby to die soon after birth.[23] This was common with lots of babies with Down syndrome, as one of the negative traits of the order is that almost half are born with atrioventricular septal defect.[24] In terms that I can understand, this is basically a hole between the receiving and sending chambers of the heart. This hole allows deoxygenated blood to mix with blood that has just gotten all freshened-up with a new load of oxygen. When this happens, only partially oxygenated blood is sent out to the rest of the body, with the net affect being that the cells counting on fresh oxygen aren't getting what they need to succeed.[25] Many Down's babies, especially prior to the current possibilities of open heart surgery, succumbed to death from this condition before they had a chance at life. Ironically, Roy Rogers and Dale Evans had a baby daughter born with Down syndrome who succumbed to this deformed heart condition as a two year old. Dale wrote a short inspirational book about this episode in their lives, as told from the view point of their daughter Robin.[26]

Tom did not have this condition or if he did, it was not severe enough to cause any long term detriment. Nonetheless, this did not hinder the recommendation that the medical profession gave Mom and Dad to give up their son before they became attached to him.

"Your son will almost certainly die at a young age." That was the frequently heard mantra.

It was bewildering, frustrating, and confusing for my folks to hear all of this and wonder what they should do. Fortunately, another doctor offered a differing opinion. He encouraged Mom and Dad with this simple, earth shaking advice: "Take your son home and just love him." Which they did.

Euthanizing infants seems like such a barbaric, medieval practice, yet it was still common practice even in the late 1940s for the medical profession to withhold care or nourishment for these "at risk" babies. Even as late as 1982 there was a celebrated legal case in Bloomington, Indiana, where the parents of a baby born with Down syndrome and a correctable medical issue did not want the child to live. They instructed the presiding doctor and medical staff to withhold nourishment with the intended result to be the death of the baby.[27] A similar case in England occurred in 1980, except that the Down's baby was totally healthy. The medical staff consented to those parents' wishes to withhold nourishment and the baby died. The doctor was tried for murder, but was eventually acquitted.[28]

This attitude was a vestige of a philosophy from the late 1800s through the mid-1900s called eugenics. It advocated for a society free from the burdens of feeble-mindedness, low intelligence, and crime, all of which were thought to be inextricably linked.[29] To achieve that goal, laws were enacted in this country (and other advanced countries) to allow forced sterilization, immigration restrictions directed at specific nationalities and races, impounding in asylums, and in some cases euthanasia.[30] The Eugenics Society was made up of many prominent figures including past presidents of the United States and prime ministers of England. The society claimed that Caucasians were genetically superior to other races and that measures to curtail intrusions into their culture by the "less fit" were justified for the survival and advancement of the species. In the 1930s and '40s, it reached its most grotesque conclusion with the National Socialists in Germany and the extermination of peoples not meeting the fitness requirements of the Nazi regime.[31] Jews, Slavs, Gypsies, the developmentally disadvantaged, and homosexuals were targeted and brutally slaughtered by the millions to help build a "better world."

Thank you, Mom and Dad (as well as divine intervention) for your welcoming response in bringing Tom home to be an integral part of our family.

In his first few weeks, Tom had a hard time getting used to just being a baby. With poor muscle tone and a large tongue, he didn't have a strong sucking instinct, so he had an extra hard time taking nourishment. He became seriously dehydrated at one point. He finally got the hang of things, though, and fought his way out of that predicament.

He got whooping cough, croup, the measles, and chicken-pox, and all the regular childhood diseases. With him, though, each illness had a significantly higher mortality rate than for normal children. It seems like he was congested all the time and that Vick's VapoRub vapors were always filling his bedroom. His nasal sinuses would plug to the gills such that he'd only be able to breathe through his mouth until a monumental sneeze would clear things out. Tom's sneezes were not polite "achoos" but rather five alarm emergencies. I will not go into further details other than to say that one of Tom's sneezing events sent everyone skittering for the nearest Kleenex box, napkin, paper towel, or any handy absorbent material.

Hepatitis A is a serious disease but usually not life threatening. Tom not only got it once, but twice. Usually the first bout generates enough antibodies to prevent a relapse, but not for Tom. About a year after the bell rang ending round one, round two began.

Hepatitis A is a virus that is usually spread through ingestion of infected fecal material. It can be spread in a number of ways, but in group settings like Tom's it is usually from poor hygiene and not very thorough hand washing after using the toilet. I'm not sure if Tom got the message the first time, but after the second occurrence, he became the world's most determined hand washer. Any time Tom washed his hands, hundreds of gallons of water were consumed and he'd stand there patting or gently rubbing his fingers together under the running water, occasionally touching the bar of soap on the counter as needed.

After the second occurrence of Hepatitis, his health was pretty good for the next twenty years (if you don't consider losing one's teeth and hair a real health issue). He was between forty-five and fifty when he started having chronic problems with pneumonia, which landed him in the local hospital on a regular basis. Each time he'd get sick, it seemed like it was a little worse and the medical staff became very concerned. His lungs would be seriously compromised and he'd be on some stout antibiotics and anti-inflammatory drugs. We got fairly regular updates on his condition. His lungs became obstructed and the oxygen level in his blood dipped to dangerous levels before he started improving. We knew when he was almost well when the reports from the hospital staff included messages that he was clandestinely raiding the nurse's lounge.

He went on foraging outings to find all kinds of wonderful snacks in their break refrigerators; sandwiches, leftover pizza, yogurt, and soft drinks. It didn't matter if Tom was hooked up to an IV stand or not, because he just waltzed down the hall rolling the intra-venous set-up right along with him. Usually his escapades took place at night when things were quieter. Eventually the hospital staff learned to have Tom's room assignment be immediately outside of the nurse's station. After a couple of years of visits to the hospital floor, the regular staff knew him on a first name basis. They could also identify him by his white fanny poking out behind a flapping medical gown as he strode forth on his grazing missions.

Almost every year we went through the same drill. "Tom's back in the hospital," Mom would relay on the phone.

One of the last times it was particularly bad. He ended up in the intensive care unit because his condition was not improving. During the day his pulse-oxygen level would improve, only to badly deteriorate at night. The medical staff were attentive and were doing what they knew how to do. One of the nurses who had been a Navy corpsman prior to coming to Ames took me aside one day and confided that he was not doing his job very well with Tom. Mike (not his real name) said that normally he could work with cool, unemotional, clinical efficiency. With Tom, though, he was getting way too emotionally involved. I don't know if his confession was because he felt good or bad about himself but it was moving to see not just him, but the whole medical team pulling for Tommy.

One night it was reported that Tom had stopped breathing all together. The nurse was able to start his breathing but then Tom would stop again. Off-again-on-again all through the night, Mike kept stirring Tom so that he'd breathe. The next day the doctor gave permission for Tom to enter hospice care. It looked like the end was in sight and we were all steeling ourselves for Tom's death.

I remember going in early that next morning just as Mike was finishing up his shift and asked how things were going. He said not much better but he had gotten the idea in the night that maybe Tom was suffering from sleep apnea and perhaps that could be the cause of his suspended breathing. Obstructive sleep apnea is a common problem with Down's persons, so why someone hadn't put the pieces of the puzzle together sooner is a bit of a mystery. After conferring with the doctor, Tom was subsequently fitted with a full bi-level positive airway pressure (BiPAP) mask augmented with pure oxygen. This apparatus forced oxygenated air past the soft-tissue blockage in his throat to keep him breathing regularly while he slept. Within twenty-four hours, The Bub was back.

Tom learned to sleep with his mask like a pro. By morning it would often be scrunched on his face, but episodes with pneumonia disappeared with his improved breathing. This significantly increased his quality of life. We all took a deep breath too, as our quality of life improved with his.

Maybe the biggest bullets Tom dodged were not physical ailments. Many of the missiles fired at him had payloads of rejection and abandonment along with their sidekicks of derision, condescension, and pity. I don't know if any ever hit him, or if they did, how much damage they actually inflicted.

I wish I could say the same for myself. I've been hit too many times by bullets that, unfortunately, hit most of us as we ride in the saddle of life chasing after something. Projectiles that are issued from the mouth or eyes, sometimes from the people we know and love the best. A comment, either spoken or perfectly communicated that says, "That was the stupidest thing I've ever heard!" Or that special look that connotes, "You Jerk!" or maybe that pseudo-consoling comment, "You tried your best." (With the hidden meaning of "and you just weren't good enough.")

If Tom was hit by any of these bullets, it didn't seem to affect him in any discernable way. It is hard for me to believe that he didn't feel these shots, but it is equally amazing that he never had a need for retaliation, retribution, or worse, reflexive despondency. Tommy never seemed to carry any sense of failure or limitation that has from time to time devastated me. He exhibited no self-pity, no self-loathing, and no brooding contempt. In short, not a single manifestation of him being hurt in any way. How gifted is that? He was like a self-healing human. There is a reason that I envied Tom for his ability to not have to bear the burden of his own frailty, failure, and misgivings. Sometimes I have wondered if that extra gene he carried around with him was actually a marker of a higher standard of life.

His death came a couple of years following his getting rigged-up with the BiPAP. It was so characteristic of him the way he finally slipped away. He went like a falling row of dominos in slow motion, and without the stress of slowly suffocating in a hospital or hospice bed.

His eye doctor had been keeping tabs on cataracts that had been developing over a couple of years and finally in March of 2008 ordered surgery for him. It is a fast, painless procedure and improves one's vision remarkably. Typically, one eye is done and then a few weeks later, the second eye has its cataract removed.

Tom had a successful operation and still had a patch on one eye while he was in the waiting period for surgery on his second one. His group residence was attending a party at a place that had a set of stairs to a basement recreation area. Tom was usually good on stairs, taking them carefully one at a time, using handrails and going slowly. However, with his slightly impaired vision, he missed the bottom step, fell, and fractured a bone in his leg. He had a cast placed on it and everything seemed to be going pretty well for several days.

The phone rang and startled us awake at 4:30 in the morning. Dad was on the line saying that Tom had passed away during the night sometime probably between 3:00 and 4:00 a.m. Dot and I quickly got dressed and met Jeff and the folks at Tom's residence before the emergency medical technicians could wheel him out on a gurney to the ambulance without awakening his housemates to the incident. The family spent a few minutes in his room with his lifeless body. A lifetime of memories congealed into one big blob while I wiped away my tears and the snot running over my lips.

Tom's death certificate states that his death was the result of an embolism—a blood clot lodged in his heart. It had probably traveled from his leg fracture, which resulted from a fall down the steps, triggered by compromised vision due to his recent cataract surgery. It was like a slinky going down a set of stairs.

Tom died in his sleep on April 29, 2008. At his memorial service, two hundred people were in attendance. There were folks from out of town, leaders of the community, friends, family, neighbors, and probably fifty of his best friends from various residential facilities around the area. There was one of the most rousing, robust, and heartfelt renditions of "Jesus Loves Me" I think I will ever hear. It wasn't exactly on tune, but a sweeter sound will never be made. I tried to give a short eulogy but could barely put two sentences together. This was especially difficult after following my sister, who sang the tune Ethel Waters immortalized, "His Eye is on the Sparrow." Nancy has a lovely mezzo soprano voice and I have no idea how she could sing at all, let alone give such a beautiful tribute to Tom. While she sang, I had to keep telling myself, "Don't get emotional. You can do this. Don't listen to her. You can get through this." I didn't make it.

Tom lived a long life. It's not a record, but fifty-eight is good for anyone, let alone someone who started out on the rocky side. When Tom was born in 1949, the average age for a person with Down syndrome was twenty. It is now about sixty. For only being able to put, on his best day, four or five syllables together, he had a lot to say and was able to communicate it effectively. I still hear his voice and his unassuming homilies ramble through my head when I take the time to listen. I learned a lot of things from my brother, like:

- Speed and efficiency are overrated. It's okay to slow down. If you're driving, it's not a sin to let people pass you. It's even okay to drive under the speed limit (horror of horrors). Enjoy the ride. You'll get there when you get there; your life won't be cut short even if you're late. Take a different route on your way to work. Who cares if it takes five minutes longer? If you're not dashing to the emergency room, what's the point of all the hubbub?
- Competition is only good to a point. What is achieved with all of this "me first" business? So long as you have donuts and coffee and some pant legs to tuck into your socks, life is good. Enjoy other people's success. Their success is also yours.
- Persistence pays. You don't have to be a pest to be persistent. Gently reminding people of your needs and desires is fine. It is especially effective when you can look the potential donor in the eye, smile, genuinely crinkle your eyes in gratitude, and enthusiastically petition for your next meal of pancakes.
- Play on a swing set or dance every day. You've got to do something that feeds the soul. Doing something mindless isn't necessarily counterproductive. Being attuned to the delight of the present moment is to understand grace.
- Learn to live one day at a time. This doesn't mean not planning, but dwelling on the future (or the past) denies the pleasure and purpose of right now, down to the air

that comes with each breath, not to mention the sweetness of a good marshmallow.

- You don't have to be beautiful to be attractive. Given half a chance, people respond to gentleness, kindness, and sincerity. Intimacy is a matter of the heart, not the flesh. When you show that you really like somebody, it completely overshadows the transience of physical beauty.
- Everybody has a gift. How egocentric and arrogant to think that another person's disability prohibits them from sharing wonderful gifts with the community. We don't make our society better by expunging the different, but by including them. Why? Because everyone is a wild combination of normal and abnormal, so who is to be the judge?
- Things don't need to be equal to be equitable. Satisfaction comes from being satisfied, not over satisfied. If you don't receive as much as the next person, it's okay. There are plenty who don't receive as much as you do.
- Everyone counts. No exceptions. We live in a small world in an immense universe and we're all important.

Like all great men, Tom's legacy lives beyond the bounds of death. I frequently run into people around town that knew and loved him. We share a story or anecdote about him and then usually have a good laugh. Even death, I'm afraid, did not get much satisfaction.

Our family still gets together at Perkins on Tom's birthday to celebrate his life by ordering pancakes smothered in butter and syrup.

CHAPTER 14

Take Two

It has been several months since I wrote what I thought was the last chapter of this book. I got discouraged with the editing process so I finally just dropped everything in despair. After all, I'm not a writer. I'm an architect. I don't design words and phrases, I design buildings, places, and environments. This nit-picky, piddly, word-by-word, hand-to-hand combat with tenses, words, syntax, and grammar is way too much work. Every time I reread the story, it seemed to get duller.

So, I dropped this memoir and forgot about it—until this morning.

I woke up about 1:30 in bed feeling hot, so I grabbed my pillow and headed into the spare bedroom and jumped under some lighter weight blankets. I quickly fell back to sleep. Then I had this wonderfully vivid dream:

I was in a large city park with a large plaza and lots of people. It was summertime and there was an orchestra playing and people were dancing on a huge patio. The dancing was all spontaneous and anybody could go out and do their thing. There was a lot of variety of dancers enjoying the warm late summer afternoon. I even danced a little. Some were dancing as couples, with others just jiving to the music solo.

There was a couple, though, that stood out in that they were great dancers. It looked like they had been classically trained in ballet, but were moving improvisationally to the music like the rest of us, just with a lot more expression and gracefulness.

I don't recall what he looked like, but I remember her. She was stunningly beautiful. This young woman was in her early twenties. She was tall and lithe with shapely legs and long expressive fingers. Her brunette hair was pulled back into a pony tail revealing a beautiful face with delicate ears. She wore a simple red house dress to her knees with a waist band tied behind her back in a neat bow. I think she was barefoot. There was nothing pretentious about this naturally attractive, obviously talented young woman.

When she moved, it was like her feet never touched the ground. She glided or flew through space. Energy and grace flowed through her as she twisted and twirled and moved in the most unaffected fashion. Everything was totally relaxed as her body parted the space around her, sometimes with her dance partner, sometimes alone.

At first, many people looked at her derisively and even jeered her because she was so good and made everyone else look so bad. I could even hear some people booing. She kept dancing, virtually unaware of the negative vibes attacking her. As she danced, however, it became apparent that she was not moving to impress anyone, but just because it was so much a part of her to move to the music. As she continued to move with her pony tail bouncing along, the crowds' demeanor began to change. Derision gave way to admiration and then adulation. It made no difference to her dancing as she continued calmly and effortlessly.

The day was wearing on and it was turning a little darker. It was almost dusk and I had gone inside a small screened pavilion for some refreshment, but I could still see this woman halfway across the park. She was still dancing, but now she was the only dancer on the plaza with thousands of eyes watching her. The orchestra started playing something from Tchaikovsky's "Swan Lake."

It was a little hard to see her now because of the distance, the onset of darkness, and looking through a wire window screen, but she was still there, completely enrapturing a now enchanted crowd. She seemed to be imparting new passion and energy even to the musicians as they played with increasing emotion. The music ended and everyone erupted in cheers and applause, and then everyone rushed toward her.

She walked in my direction and stepped into the door of the pavilion where I was seated, made eye contact with me, then turned around and ran back out onto the plaza.

I startled myself awake and sat up straight in bed. My eyes wide open, mind clear. The digital clock in the corner glowed 4:10 a.m.

"TOM?!"

REFERENCES

1. National Down Syndrome Society. [Online] [Cited: January 15, 2015.] http://www.ndss.org/Down-Syndrome/ Down-Syndrome-Facts.

2. Wright, David. *Downs, The History of a Disability*. New York : Oxford University Press, 2011. pp. 49-52.

3. —. *Downs, The History of a Disability*. New York : Oxford University Press, 2011. p. 52.

4. —. *Downs, The History of a Disability*. New York : Oxford University Press, 2011. pp. 116-118.

5. —. *Downs, The History of a Disability*. New York : Oxford University Press, 2011. p. 123.

6. —. *Downs, The History of a Disability*. New York : Oxford University Press, 2011. p. 10.

7. —. *Downs, The History of a Disability*. New York : Oxford University Press, 2011. pp. 154-158.

8. Records, Peter Pan, [prod.]. Popeye. [78 RPM vinyl record] s.l. : The Peter Pan Orchestra and Chorus, No date.

9. Records, Golden, [prod.]. Superman. [78 RPM vinyl record] s.l. : The Video Singers and Orchestra, No date.

10. Pickard, Bethan Mair. *Music and Down's Syndrome*. [Online] 2009. Unpublished work, Royal Welsh College of Music and Drama, University of Wales. http://www.riverbendds.org/index. htm?page=pickard.html

11. Schalkwijk, F.W. *Music and People with Developmental Disabilities: Music Therapy, Remedial Music Making and Musical Activities.*

London : Jessica Kingsley Publishers, 1994. p. 14. As referenced in
Pickard Web article, "music and Down's Syndrome".

12. *Rhythm and Time in Perception of Down's Syndrome Children.*
Stratford, B. and Ching, E.Y. 1, 1983, Journal of Medical
Deficiency Research, Vol. 27, p. 37. As cited in Pickard Web article.

13. Understanding Hepatitus A and/or Hepatitus B.
HelpPreventDisease.com. [Online] http://helpreventdisease.com/
adult_vaccines/vaccines-preventable-hepatitus/understanding-
hepatitis-aand-b.html

14. Wright, David. *Downs, The History of a Disability.* New York :
Oxford University Press, 2011. p. 185.

15. Rothman, David and Rothman, Sheila. *The Willowbrook Wars,
Bringing the Mentally Disabled into the Community.* New Brunswick :
Transaction Publishers, 2005. pp. 260-267. Originally published
by Harper and Row in 1984

16. *Museum of Disability.* [Online] http://museumofdisability.org/
virtual-museum/medicine-wing/medicine-timeline-exhibit/

17. Wright, David. *Downs, The History of a Disability.* New York :
Oxford University Press, 2011. p. 135.

18. Blatt, Burton and Kaplan, Fred. *Christmas in Purgatory, A
Photographic Essay on Mental Retardation.* Syracuse : s.n., 1974.

19. Rothman, David and Rothman, Sheila. *The Willowbrook Wars,
Bringing the Mentally Disabled into the Community.* New Brunswick :
Transaction Publishers, 2005. p. 16. Originally published by
Harper and Row in 1984.

20. List of Motor Vehicle Deaths in U.S. by year. *Wikipedia.* [Online]
http://en.wikipedia.org/wiki/List of motor vehicle deaths in U.S.
by year.

21. Wright, David. *Downs, The History of a Disability.* New York :
Oxford University Press, 2011. pp. 141-143.

22. McGuire, Dennis. If People with Down Syndrome Ruled
the World. [Online] Speech presented to National Down
Syndrome Society conference in Chicago, IL in 2005.
http://www.dsamn.org/wp-content/uploads/2012/03/
IfPeoplewithDownSyndromeRuledthe World.pdf

23. Wright, David. *Downs, The History of a Disability.* New York : Oxford University Prress, 2011. pp. 162-163.

24. —. *Downs, The History of a Disability.* New York : Oxford University Press, 2011. pp. 161-162.

25. Atrioventricula Septal Defect definition. *Wikipedia.* [Online] http://en.wikipedia.org/wiki/Atrioventricular septal defect.

26. Rogers, Dale Evans. *Angel Unaware.* 8th Printing. Grand Rapids : Flemming H. Revell, 1998.

27. Wright, David. *Downs, The History of a Disability.* New York : Oxford University Press, 2011. p. 164.

28. —. *Downs, The History of a Disability.* New York : Oxford University Press, 2011. p. 165.

29. *Museum of Disability.* [Online] http://museumofdisability.org/virtual-museum/societyo-wing/eugenics-exhibit.

30. *Museum of Disability.* [Online] http://museumofdisability.org/virtual-museum/medicine-wing/medicine-timeline-exhibit/

31. Wright, David. *Downs, The History of a Disability.* New York : Oxford University Press, 2011. pp. 162-163.